earth

L I M I T E D

50 SIMPLE THINGS YOUR BUSINESS CAN DO TO SAVE THE PLANET

THE EARTHWORKS GROUP

GREENLEAF PUBLISHING
in association with **CAPITB plc**
1993

Earth Limited
50 Simple Things Your Business Can Do to Save the Planet

Originally published in the USA as
50 Simple Things Your Business Can Do to Save the Earth
The Earth Works Group

Copyright © 1991 by the Earthworks Press Inc.
All Rights Reserved

Published in the UK by Greenleaf Publishing in
association with CAPITB plc.

Greenleaf Publishing is an imprint of
Interleaf Productions Limited
Sidney Street, Sheffield S1 3QF
England

Typeset by Interleaf Productions Limited
Printed on environmentally friendly, acid-free paper
from managed forests using water-based soya ink
by The Cromwell Press, Melksham, Wiltshire

British Library Cataloguing in Publication Data

Earthworks Group
Earth Limited:50 Simple Things Your
Business Can Do to Save the Planet
I. Title
658.4
ISBN 1-874719-10-1

Contents

Foreword

The challenge of achieving sustainable development is one of the most important and difficult facing us today. The business community has a vital role to play, for only it can actually deliver much of the practical action that is needed to protect the environment.

Businesses have to plan ahead and can see more readily the need to protect future markets by ensuring that we use the world's resources in a way which doesn't harm the opportunities for the next generation.

Business already faces environmental pressures from tightening legislation and the demands of the market place; in the future the environment will become a key competitive issue. The environment also offers huge business opportunities for those companies who adopt a positive approach.

I am aware that many companies are already developing comprehensive environmental strategies. However, I also know that this is only part of the picture—small and medium-sized companies find it harder to keep abreast of developments in the environmental field and to determine how to take the first steps towards improving their environmental performance. This publication can help by providing practical examples of simple, effective measures that businesses can take to improve their environmental performance. It doesn't just say *why* businesses should do something, it actually says *what* they can do.

I hope this publication will encourage more companies to respond positively to the challenge posed by the environment.

John Gummer,
Secretary of State for the Environment,
October 1993

Acknowledgements

Caroline Aistrop ● Wildfowl and Wetlands Trust

Colin Ashford ● Building Research Establishment

Kim Betty ● British Airways

Robin Bines ● BIS Strategic Decisions

John Brooks ● DTI Environmental Helpline

Jonathon Cattell ● Environ

Edwin Datschefski ● Environment Council

Diane Farrell ● The Lane Group

Pip Frankish ● 3M

Keith Hall ● Association of Environment Conscious Building

Sue Hall ● Waste Watch

John Hamilton ● CAPITB plc

Hugh King ● Thorn Lighting

Dr Alan Knight ● B & Q

Leslie Millett ● Waste Busters

Geoff Mills ● Alexander Gibb

Tony Muldoon ● Enterprise Plants

Anne Marie O'Connor ● Jupiter Tyndau Merlin

Catherine Oliver ● BIS Strategic Decisions

Ivy Penman ● Exel Logistics

Mike Samuel ● Sainsbury's

John Sauven ● Greenpeace and Friends of the Earth

Doug Teesdale ● Paper Recycling Company

Mike Thornton ● LEEP

Dr Chris Tuppen ● British Telecom

Jacquie Verbeek ● World Wide Fund for Nature

Dr David Wheeler ● Bodyshop

Teresa White ● Action Resource Centre

Researched for the UK market by John Stuart

Cartoons by Mike Flanagan

Introduction

Everyone in business—regardless of the position you hold in your company—has considerable influence over what happens to the environment. Each of you has a say in decisions that directly affect the state of the Earth. . . and the way people feel about taking care of it.

If, for example, you're responsible for purchasing supplies or products, you influence your vendors. Should they provide products that are better for the planet? You can help them decide by using your economic clout.

If you have a hand in building your company's image, you influence the way management—and the rest of the company—feels about the environment. Do people really care? Are they really getting the message? You can use your communications skills to spread the word.

If you manage production, you may be able to choose between toxic and non-toxic materials, and to influence methods of disposal.

If you work in an office, a workshop, a factory, you are the backbone of your company. You and co-workers can use your collective influence to mould policy decisions.

Of course, each of you has decisions to make each day. Should you throw out that piece of paper...or recycle it? Is it too much trouble to wash out a mug so you don't have to use a disposable cup? Should you leave a light or a copier running...or turn it off?

But in the end, it comes down to something quite simple: Business success is directly linked to the health of the Earth and its resources, including human resources. By taking some of the positive steps outlined in this book, you'll be making an investment in the future.

The payoff on this investment isn't necessarily long-term. As you'll see, many of the ideas described in this book can yield dividends in this fiscal year—in cost savings, lower taxes, improved company image, and in increased employee satisfaction and productivity. This is a textbook case of 'doing well by doing good'.

Not all of these 'simple things' will be right for your company. Big companies' needs are different from small companies'; businesses which own their own facilities have different needs from those that lease them; and industrial companies have different needs from retail and service businesses.

And you probably won't be able to implement more than a few of these things at once. In fact, if you take on too many 'simple things' right away, you may lack the resources and support to make them work. So take it slowly, one idea at a time. As you build experience and confidence, other steps will follow naturally and easily.

We recognize the realities of business and know it's not possible to turn well-honed products and processes topsy-turvy to protect the environment and still function as a business. But we have no doubt that being an environmentally responsible corporate citizen will give you a competitive advantage in the market place for years to come, and we know you want to save the Earth.

The Earth Works Group,
Berkeley, California

1 Mug Shot

In Britain we throw away enough paper and plastic cups to circle the equator more than 14 times.

You take one last sip of coffee and throw the cup into the rubbish bin. Now it's time to get down to work. Sound familiar? It probably does—the average British worker goes through around 500 disposable cups every year.

The Disposable Blues

- All those empty cups don't just disappear. Plastic cups are made from either foamed or hard-walled polystyrene—which never decomposes, no matter where you dump it.

- Paper cups don't break down easily, either. In fact, in a landfill—where most disposables end up—almost nothing breaks down. It just sits there.

- Both types of disposables use resources and create pollution. For example, polystyrene is made from a carcinogenic oil by-product called benzene. Paper cups are bleached, a process which puts toxic dioxins into our waterways.

- Plastic cups are touted by the plastics industry as 'recyclable'. Technically, that's true but until recently there weren't any companies involved in their recovery. Cups don't get recycled into more cups—so recycling doesn't reduce pollution or resource consumption.

Simple Things To Do

- Consider issuing each employee with a ceramic mug; perhaps your company logo or an environmental message could be printed on the side.

- Or keep sturdy mugs, not plastic cups, near the office teapot or eating area.

- Don't buy plastic stirrers - just keep some spoons on hand.

- If there's space to wash dishes, consider making durable plastic dishes available for employee use.

- Arrange for your cafeteria or canteen to give a discount to employees who bring their own mug when buying a cup of tea or coffee.

- Arrange with owners of nearby take-aways to give discounts to employees who bring their own mugs. If they have a salad bar, see if they'll let employees bring their own dishes or plastic containers instead of using the take-away's disposable dishes.

- If ceramic mugs aren't practical, make sure you're using hard-walled plastic disposable cups and contact Save-a-Cup Recycling Company Ltd. They're a unique non-profit-making company who will provide equipment and expertise to enable you to recycle your disposables.

Success Story

✔ Save-a-Cup give awards each quarter for the best recyclers. One recipient, Honeywell Control Systems in Bracknell, improved their collection figures by 48.9% because of improved internal publicity. The facility of 450 employees now recycles about a ton and a half of plastic a year—360,000 cups.

The Bottom Line

For Your Company

✍ High quality ceramic mugs cost about £1.65 each in bulk (including your company logo). Plastic cups cost about £5.40 per year per employee. Assuming each person uses only two per day, but most employees use more than that, mugs will pay for themselves in about four months.

✍ Recycling your plastic cups won't save your company anything—but it will demonstrate to staff your commitment to sustainability.

For the Earth

✍ If a million people used their own mugs in the office each day, or recycled their disposables, we could eliminate as many as $1^1/_4$ billion cups from going to landfill. Lined up end to end, that's a saving of around 360 feet of landfill space per person per year—a total of some 75,000 miles of rubbish.

Resources

■ Save-a-Cup Recycling Company Ltd, Suite 2, Bridge House, Bridge Street, High Wycombe, Bucks HP11 2EL. 0494 510167.

■ Greenpeace Merchandise, Kingsway, Gateshead, Tyne and Wear NE11 0NE. 091 491 0033. *They sell mugs printed with environmental messages.*

■ Chris Ashton Ceramics, The Pottery, 4 High Street, Eckesley, Nr. Retford, Notts DN22 8AJ. 0777 838391. *They sell mugs in bulk which can be printed with your company logo.*

■ Check in the Yellow Pages under catering or pottery supplies for local sources of mugs.

2 Success On a Plate

660 million meals were served to British business and industry in 1992.

I sn't it amazing how much rubbish is left after you eat a canteen lunch? There's a small mound of napkins, cups, utensils, plates, wrappers, coffee stirrers and so on—and that doesn't even include the leftover food.

But it doesn't take a lot of effort to trim your canteen's 'waste-line'. The results can be good for your company's bottom line, too.

Out to Lunch

■ Restaurants and other food service institutions create about 8% of Britain's municipal waste—almost 3 million tons a year.

■ According to a recent study, typical cafeteria waste consists of: paper 40%, food 23%, plastic 13%, polystyrene foam 10%, tin 8%, glass 5% and aluminium 1%.

■ It is estimated that more than $^1/_3$ of this waste is recyclable.

■ That includes the food. Some companies are beginning to compost their leftovers, which keeps them out of landfills.

Simple Things to Do

In the Company Cafeteria

■ Reduce packaging. Check with vendors to see if your cafeteria's purchases can be delivered in fewer, larger cartons.

■ Buy recycled and unbleached paper products—towels, napkins, coffee filters, etc. Bleaching can produce dioxins, which pollute water and may leave traces in the paper.

■ Whenever possible, use re-usable plates, cups and cutlery. Disposables are a last resort, but if you buy them, check to see what can be recycled locally.

- Use soft drink, milk, cream and condiment dispensers instead of individual cans, cartons and packets.

- If you use cans, invest in a can-crusher.

- Make sure your equipment is properly maintained and turn it off when it's not in use.

- If you're buying new equipment invest in ovens or hobs with better energy efficiency ratings.

- Donate excess food to a local shelter for the homeless or needy.

- Post your 'cafeteria environmental policy' where everyone can see it.

- Encourage recycling, keep bins handy so employees can easily recycle after eating. Let employees bring recyclables from home; it can help your recycling centre break even—or even make a profit.

Work with Local Restaurants

- When you have food delivered to meetings, ask restaurants not to include disposables. Use your own utensils, etc.

Success Story

✔ ICL, who manufacture computers, have a 'green' notice-board in their reception area to give employees up-to-date information on recycling and environmental issues. In their cafeteria all equipment is regularly maintained and switched off when not in use. All bottles, cans, plastic cups and stirrers are recycled and the napkins used are made from recycled paper.

The company, in liaison with their contractor, is aiming to reduce the use of disposables and cut down on chemicals used for cleaning.

The Bottom Line

For Your Company

✍ You probably won't save any money here. The biggest benefit from creating a 'green' canteen is what it does for your company's image—and employees' self-image. Of course, there's a possibility that costs may be offset through reduced waste disposal costs and canteen recycling programmes—but there's no guarantee.

For the Earth

✍ Re-using and recycling saves resources. If half of all company canteens and restaurants reduced their waste by just 10%, we could eliminate over 100,000 tons of waste a year.

Resources

■ Hotel and Catering Institutional Management Association, 191 Trinity Road, London SW17 7HN. 081 672 4251.

■ Business Green, P.O. Box 27, Liphook, Hants GU30 7UB. 0428 725150. *Provide a commercial environmental assessment and practical advice for the hotel and tourist industry.*

■ The Westminster Initiative, 9th Floor, Westminster City Hall, 64 Victoria Street, London SW1 6QP. 071 798 3402. *Send SAE with 34p stamp (Oct. 1993 rate) for the 'Considerate Restauranteurs Handbook'.*

3 Copy Right

In Britain we make nearly 500 billion photocopies a year—about 930,000 copies every minute of every day.

No doubt about it—we are 'copy-holics'. Our fingers itch at the thought of running off copies of everything from newspaper articles to inter-office memos. Yes, we've all seen the bins overflowing with unwanted copies—but we just can't control ourselves—we've *got* to make *just one more copy*. Well, don't panic. There's help for our habit.

Copy Mania

According to BIS Strategic Decisions, there were more than 850,000 copiers in operation in the United Kingdom in 1990. By 1995, it is estimated there will be in excess of 1 million.

According to one expert, the average 100-person company uses about 250,000 sheets of copier paper a year. That's a stack of paper stretching nearly five floors high.

Simple Things to Do

Save Paper

- ■ Try copying on both sides of the paper. It could cut your paper use in half.

- ■ Keep a collection box next to the copier for discarding bad copies. Put a sign near the copier asking employees to use the box.

- ■ Use the discards as scrap or send them to your recycling centre.

- ■ Use recycled copier paper. A growing number of office supply stores stock it.

Save Energy

- ■ If the machine is used infrequently, turn it off when it's not in use. Even an idle copier uses a surprising amount of electricity.

- If your copier is often on all night, consider getting a timer that will shut the machine off between, say, 8 p.m. and 8 a.m.

If You're Buying a Copier

- Look into duplex machines (which do two-sided copying).

- Investigate a copier with a zoom feature. These can automatically reduce four A4 originals onto one sheet, cutting paper use by 75%.

- Select a copier with a power-saver feature. It can cut energy use considerably by incorporating an auto-switch-off mode, timer switch and fast warm-up facility. (This will also reduce ozone emissions.)

Success Story

✔ The Institute of Wastes Management have had high-speed duplex copiers for a couple of years. It is now policy to use double-sided copying for all reports, minutes and documents. According to personnel officer Linda Rogers, the Institute has made major savings on paper usage and more than justified the purchase price.

The Bottom Line

For Your Company

£ You can cut copier paper usage by as much as 50%. If your company makes 5,000 copies a month, cutting paper use in half would save 30,000 sheets a year, or about £300 worth of paper.

£ Energy-efficiency measures can save even more money. (See Turn It Off, page 58).

For the Earth

£ If each copier in the UK used five fewer copies every business day, we could save up to 2.5 million reams of paper. That would save the equivalent of 200,000 trees and keep more than 3.7 million cubic feet of paper out of landfills.

£ If just 10% of our office copiers had power-saving features — or were simply turned off when not in use—we could save an estimated billion kilowatt hours of electricity, the energy equivalent of 570,000 barrels of oil a year.

Resources

■ Try a local paper distributor. If they don't have recycled copier paper, contact:

■ Universal Office Supplies, Tameside Drive, Holford, Birmingham B6 7AY. 021 6260011.

■ The Green Business Company, Studio One, 114 Walcot Street, Bath BA1 5BG. 0225 480556.

4 Just the Fax

According to Erskine (one of the biggest fax suppliers in Britain) there are now over 1 million fax machines in use in the UK.

'I'll fax it to you' has become as much a part of British business as 'Your cheque is in the post.' It seems that just about everyone has access to a facsimile machine these days—so everyone has to cope with those curled-up pieces of shiny paper coming in at all hours of the day and night. Faxing itself isn't bad. It uses less energy than other methods of sending documents and eliminates the need for envelopes, labels and stamps. But it's how you fax that makes the difference.

Fax Facts

- Fax use in the UK increased by 33% in the number of faxes sent and 38% in the number of documents received according to preliminary findings in Gallup's 1993 fax use and application survey.

- Unfortunately, standard fax paper isn't generally recyclable. It's coated with chemicals that are heated to create the printed images on a fax. These chemicals contaminate the recycling process.

    Because the chemicals deteriorate, faxes can fade after about six months. To save them, people often make photocopies —which wastes even more paper.

    Experts estimate that about one in four faxes gets photocopied.

Simple Things to Do

- Buy a plain paper fax. They work like photocopiers or laser printers; the faxes come out on plain paper and don't fade—which eliminates extra photocopying and enables you to recycle unwanted faxes. They aren't cheap—some sell for over £2,000—but prices are expected to drop and Group 3 models are now available for as little as £900.

- Buy recycled thermal fax paper: it sells for a comparable price to your usual paper.

- Use smaller cover sheets. Instead of using a full page, use a half page. If you send five faxes a day, you'll save the equivalent of six rolls of paper in a year.

- Or don't use a cover sheet at all. You can buy 'Post-It' fax transmission stickers. Stick one on the first page before you send it.

The Bottom Line

For Your Company

- Plain paper fax machines are more expensive to buy, but less expensive to use.

- Faxes cost as little as 1.5p each, compared with 2.5p–3p for a thermal fax. But plain paper models also require toner and developer, which add to their operation cost. In the end, the cost of the two machines is pretty close—but the quality of the plain paper fax makes it a much better buy.

For the Earth

- If everyone who owns a fax machine switched from full-page to half-page cover sheets, we could save about 120,000 miles-worth of unrecyclable fax paper—without reducing the number of faxes.

- If one in 10 fax users switched to a plain paper fax, and those faxes were recycled, we could save an additional 50,000 miles-worth of paper.

Resources

Plain Paper Fax Machines

- Canon (UK) Ltd, Freepost BM1 489, Birmingham B1 1BR. Freephone 0800 252223.
  Have recently introduced a low-price plain paper fax machine.

- Toshiba Information Systems, Facsimile division, Freepost TK 842, Weybridge, Surrey KT15 2HL. 0642 460444.

- Muratec Communications Europe NV, Gatton Place, St Mathew's Road, Redhill, Surrey RH1 1TA. 0737 780178.

Recycled Fax Paper

- Infotec UK Ltd, Stirling Way, Barnet By-pass, Borehamwood, Herts WD6 2AE. 081 207 2700.

The BBC saved 11,620 kilos of paper for recycling in 1991—the equivalent of almost 2,000 trees

Courtaulds Films Cellophane have distributed 20,000 copies of their six-page environmental review to homes in the Bridgewater area—the review explains progress made to upgrade the Bridgewater factory in terms of making the company a better neighbour

Parcelforce are substantially reducing their £20 million/year fuel costs through driver training, speed limiters, aerodynamic kits and fuel keys to analyse individual vehicle performance

B&Q decided not to purchase peat from SSSIs (Sites of Special Scientific Interest) and have developed a range of peat-free alternatives

5 Flexible Friends

Britain charged about £40 billion to credit cards in 1992.

'**A**nd how will you be paying for that?' Every time you charge something on a credit card you could be using a little bit of your spending power to support environmental groups.

Charge It

■ Whenever you use your Visa or Mastercard, the retailer pays a small processing fee to the main bank involved in setting up the network.

■ Some banks have a service called 'affinity cards' which make it possible for environmental groups to get a portion of the cards' turnover. Once an environmental group signs up with the card-issuing bank, a part of each 'affinity card' purchase goes to that group. It may only be a few pence per charge, but it adds up.

■ How much? Since April 1990 the National Trust Visa Card has earned the organisation in excess of £800,000.

Simple Things to Do

■ Switch your credit card to an 'affinity card'. Contact the issuing banks for details of affinity programmes that benefit environmental groups.

■ Check with environmental organisations you want to support. See if they have an 'affinity card' programme. Many groups (e.g. RSNC—The Wildlife Trusts Partnership, The Woodland Trust, etc.) do.

■ Tell employees about 'affinity' services. They might want to switch too.

■ Watch out for the introduction of company 'affinity cards'. Several banks are looking to introduce this service as soon as is practicable.

Success Story

✔ The RSPB's Visa Card with the Co-op, introduced in 1988, now has 50,000 card holders. The RSPB receive £5 for every new account opened and $^1/4$% of turnover. The revenue from the card has now exceeded £1 million, enabling the RSPB to purchase and manage land for conservation work.

The Bottom Line

✍ Switching to affinity credit cards won't cost you much (if anything) but it can raise millions for groups working to save the earth—if Britons put just 3% of charges on affinity cards benefiting environmental groups we could boost donations by £5 million per year.

Resources

■ Co-operative Bank, P.O. Box 101, 1 Balloon Street, Manchester M60 4EP. 0345 212212. (Calls charged at local rate.)

■ Customer Information Services, Midland Bank plc, Griffin House, Silverstreet Head, Sheffield S1 1AY. 0742 528788.

■ Bank of Scotland, Card Services, Pitreavie Business Park, Dunfermline KY99 4BS. 0383 738855.

6 Cut Paper

By the year 2000, British businesses will be filing about 10 billion sheets of new paper a year—enough to fill 400,000 filing cabinets.

Maybe you didn't need to send a copy of that last memo to everybody, but you wanted to make sure no one was left out. And wouldn't you know it—the only paper handy when you had to jot down that phone number was a new piece of stationery. We all use more paper than we need to. But there are plenty of ways to cut down.

Did You Know?

■ British businesses now use about 2 million tons of paper every year. That's about 75 pounds for each man, woman and child.

■ According to one estimate more than 30 million trees are cut down each year to make office paper for the UK.

■ We throw away enough office paper every year to build a 12-foot high wall from Leeds to Edinburgh.

■ Each ton of paper thrown away can cost up to £8 to discard and takes up 3 cubic feet of landfill space. Landfill costs are expected to double by the year 2000.

■ According to Wastebusters Ltd, about 70% of all office rubbish is wastepaper that could be recycled.

Simple Things to Do

■ Use both sides of the paper. It's increasingly common for letters and reports to be written on both the front and back sides.

■ Cut down on memos. Just post a few copies where people will see them—around the canteen, in restrooms, lifts, etc.

■ Set up a bulletin board on every floor or in each department for notices and memos.

- If you have a networked computer system, consider using electronic mail for inter-office memos.

- Use scrap paper. If you have outdated letterheads, reports or other unwanted paper that's printed on one side, turn it into note paper.

Success Story

✔ Marks & Spencer have cut their consumption of paper by hundreds of tons per year by examining the validity of every single piece of paper they use. Documents were combined, paper re-used and double-sided photocopying encouraged. The annual savings are as much as $2/3$ of store turnover.

The Bottom Line

For Your Company

🖊 Using less paper costs nothing, but it can save money and waste disposal fees. If employees in a 100-person office used both sides of the paper only 10% of the time, the company could save £200 a year in reduced paper costs.

For the Earth

🖊 If all employees reduced paper use by just 5%, we could save over 100,000 tons of paper each year, enough to save about $1^1/_2$ million trees. It would also reduce the air and water pollution generated by making new paper.

For Further Information

- 'The Greenpeace Guide to Paper'. Send a cheque for £3.50 (Oct. 1993 rate) payable to: Greenpeace Merchandise, P.O. Box 10, Gateshead, Tyne & Wear NE8 1LL. You can also pay by credit card on 091 491 0034.

7 Use Greener Cleaners

Many of the chemical pollutants found in sewage systems come from institutional cleaners.

When you clean at home, you know what products you're using. But at work, everything gets clean 'magically'. When you arrive there in the morning, the rubbish has been taken out, the toilets are spotless, the floor has been scrubbed.

What about the cleaning supplies it took to get the job done? They may be harmful to the environment and to you. It's worth having your company look into it.

Dirty Business

■ Many commercial cleaning products contain toxic, corrosive or flammable chemicals like perchloroethylene, napthalene, sodium hypochlorite, toluene and benzene.

■ Many of these ingredients get washed down drains and into sewage systems. They're supposed to break down or be filtered out in waste water treatment plants, but that doesn't always happen. The result: toxins get into the water supply.

■ Many cleaners use chlorine as a disinfectant. In waste water, chlorine can react with organic and other compounds to create toxins or carcinogens.

■ That's not all. The fumes from these products also cause pollution indoors. Some irritate people's eyes, noses and lungs.

Success Stories

✔ The University of Surrey at Guildford have switched to 'Citra-clean', made from orange zest and utilising the natural solvent D-limonene. It's mainly used for cleaning toilets, enabling the university to cut out high acid products and bleach.

✔ As part of their environmental stance, Exel Logistics wanted greener cleaners at their media distribution centre. They asked contractors applying for the tender what chemicals they used. Only one, Approved Spotless Cleaning Services, had a policy—they used 'Citraclean' made from the natural solvent, D-limonene, which is now used for most jobs in different dilutions.

✔ Another D-limonene based cleaner from the Darenas 'Green Line' is used at Abbey National's headquarters in London. 'It cleans well and is in keeping with our environmental policy' says press officer Nick Salter.

✔ Hounslow Borough Council use 'Citraclean' for everything from general cleaning to de-gunking engines in their vehicle workshops. They also use 'Micro-clean', which deals with anything that's organic by eating the bacteria. It's safe to use, versatile and has cost-effectively replaced three other products for toilets and housing estate clean-ups.

Simple Things to Do

■ Use cleaners that won't harm people or the environment.

■ They aren't always available from janitorial supply firms. You may need to contact the manufacturers directly.

■ Instead of buying one product to clean floors, another for glass, etc., look for all-purpose products. They allow you to buy bigger quantities of fewer products, saving money and reducing packaging.

■ Look for concentrated cleaners. Concentrates give you more product for less packaging and use fewer resources being transported from factory to business. They usually cost less, too.

■ Provide your maintenance staff with instructions on how to use greener cleaners. Many work in a different way to traditional products (e.g. some create fewer suds) and take a little getting used to. The manufacturer will provide educational materials.

The Bottom Line

For Your Company

🖉 Greener cleaners cost more to buy than other institutional cleaning products, but because they are usually concentrated they can save money in the long run if you use them efficiently.

In the USA some contract cleaning companies are being sued by ex-employees about the health problems caused by chemicals they were exposed to. Green cleaners are safe to use.

For the Earth

🖉 Greener cleaners will cut the amount of harmful chemicals sent into the water supply.

Resources

■ Bio-Productions, Hawkhurst, Kent TN18 4XH. 0580 752462. *Makers of 'Citraclean' and 'Micro-Clean'.*

■ ISS Darenas Ltd, Daren House, Kingsbury Road, Curdworth, Sutton Coldfield, West Midlands. 0675 470670. *Suppliers of a range of green cleaning products.*

■ CMB Ltd, P.O. Box 110, Kent BR2 6ED. 081 846 9251. *Suppliers of the 'Ark' range of industrial cleaners.*

8 A Package Deal

Britain produces about 8.4 million tons of packaging waste a year— enough to fill almost 19,000 jumbo jets.

It's time to pack an order. First, pull out a new corrugated box and secure the bottom with plastic parcel tape. Now put the merchandise in a plastic bag and set it in the box; put polystyrene beads all around for protection. Finally, close the box and seal it with more tape. Don't forget to cover the address with extra tape—just in case.

Congratulations—you've just created an environmental nightmare. But don't feel boxed in; there are plenty of things you can do to clean up your packaging act.

Pack Facts

- British businesses use an estimated 6 million cubic feet of polystyrene 'beads' a year—enough to fill the Canary Wharf tower nearly three times.

- Annually we use the equivalent of 140 corrugated cardboard boxes for each person in Britain—enough to make a pile as big as a football pitch and one and a half times as high as Nelson's Column.

- Every year, Britain sends some 750 million packages through Parcelforce, TNT, Red Star and the other major carriers. That's 15 for every man, woman and child in the country.

Simple Things to Do

When You Ship

- Re-use items from old packages: envelopes, boxes, polystyrene 'beads' etc. Devise a system for collecting the 'beads' you receive; then send them on to the packing department.

- Make your own packaging materials: run non-recyclable paper through a shredder. It works well to pack delicate objects.

■ Do a packaging audit. Is everything you're using really necessary for the product's protection or are you over-packaging?

Recycled & Recyclable

■ Use paper packaging tape instead of plastic. It makes boxes easier to recycle.

■ Buy roll-ends from local printers, or newspapers for use as packing materials. Roll-ends are the final few feet of a printer's roll of paper, which can't be used and are often thrown away.

■ Re-use manilla envelopes. Get a rubber stamp that says, 'This envelope is being re-used as part of our environmental policy.'

■ Check with local recyclers. The adhesive on pressure-sensitive labels may make boxes and envelopes unsuitable for recycling.

■ Use Jiffy bags filled with recycled paper. Envelopes with bubble-pak inside are non-recyclable.

■ Enclose a note in your packages asking recipients to re-use packing materials.

Success Stories

✔ 3M have a 'Packaging and the Environment' code of practice which incorporates the three r's—reduce, re-use, and recycle. In the last two years this has led to a total reduction in packaging of 1,500 tons throughout Europe.

✔ Natural Fact, an environmentally conscious clothing company in London, cut out all packaging that is not essential. Mail-order items are shipped in simple recycled cardboard boxes.

Resources

- British Fibreboard Packaging Association/REPAK, 2 Saxon Court, Freeschool Street, Northampton NN1 1ST. 0604 21002.

- The Industry Council for Packaging and the Environment (INCPEN), Tenterden House, 3 Tenterden Street, London W1R 9AH. 071 409 0949.

Conserv-Supplies operate a 'waste responsible' policy—all waste generated from production or administration is recycled including paper, cardboard, plastic, metals and organic waste

3M Neotechnic re-used or recycled almost 90% of their waste in 1991

3M introduced '3P—Pollution Prevention Pays' in 1975 and as a result have eliminated half of all pollutants and saved over £300 million—worldwide

The Bodyshop have introduced in-store refilling and recycling systems in 1992/3. A container was refilled every 13 seconds and one returned for recycling every four seconds. About 3.4 million containers were rescued in 1992/3

9 Go Public

About 7 million workers drive to work alone every day. That's enough cars to form a convoy from London to San Francisco.

Did you drive to work this morning? How was it—was the road crowded? Were the parking fees higher than your weekly salary? Did you have to take out a second mortgage just to fill your petrol tank?

Not everyone is lucky enough to have an alternative. But if you live in an urban area, you probably have—you can go by public transport. It doesn't have all the conveniences of driving your own car, but it doesn't have the headaches either. The less you drive, the better it is for the planet.

Breathe Easier

- Commuting by public transport takes as little as $1/30$ of the energy needed to commute by car.

- Each person who uses public transport instead of a private car saves an average of 62 pounds of carbon dioxide and 5 pounds of nitrogen oxides (which contribute to acid rain) from going into the atmosphere every year.

Simple Things to Do

- Offer bus and rail passes to employees at a discount. Better yet, give them away.

- Provide an interest-free loan for bus/rail season tickets. In some companies employees pay annual loans back on a regular basis; this costs considerably less than a weekly ticket.

- Distribute copies of public transport route maps to employees. They're free from most transport companies.

■ If your company isn't close to a bus stop or railway station set up a company mini-bus (or van, or car) to take workers back and forth (see - 'Everyone into the Pool' page 96). Co-ordinate it with the arrival of buses or trains to minimise waiting times.

Success Stories

✔ The Automobile Association offer employees an interest-free loan for annual bus or rail tickets repayable over a 10-month period. The scheme has been running for many years with great success.

✔ Sainsbury's supermarkets offer annual season tickets in a free-loan scheme. About 40% of London staff now take part.

✔ Body Shop International run a twice-daily minibus service for employees between Littlehampton, Bognor Regis and Worthing, and a shuttle service to and from the local railway station.

The Bottom Line

For Your Business

✎ Reducing traffic congestion helps cut the cost of moving people and goods.

✍ Space that would be devoted to car parks can be used more profitably for other business purposes.

✍ Staff can be more productive by using public transport.

For the Earth

✍ If only 1% of UK car owners left their cars at home one day a week, it could save 14 million gallons of petrol a year and cut pollutants substantially. For example: we'd keep 200 million pounds of CO_2 out of the atmosphere.

✍ If 2% of people commuting into central London by car changed to public transport, we'd save a million hours of stop-go pollution and gain a million hours of potentially productive work time—every year.

Resource

■ Transport 2000, Walkden House, 10 Melton Street, London NW1 2EJ. 071 388 8386.

10 The Cartridge Family

British businesses throw out almost 2 million plastic toner cartridges every year, enough to stretch from London to Milan.

Y ou probably hate it when the 'low toner' light on your copier comes on, or you get to the end of your typewriter ribbon.
Not only do you get your hands dirty changing it, you have to throw away a big chunk of plastic. There ought to be something you can do with it: an art project, pencil holder, paperweight? Actually, there's a simple solution: fill it up again.

Toning Up

■ Many photocopiers and laser printers use plastic toner cartridges that must be replaced. The cartridges, which are expensive to replace, contain the toner that you see as the image on the page.

■ The plastic container doesn't wear out, it can be re-used many times. The same is true for typewriter and printer ribbons. The ribbons run out, but the plastic casings are re-usable.

■ Laser printer and copier cartridges weigh 3–4 pounds each. That means about 4,000 tons of plastic cartridges end up in landfills every year, not including print ribbon cartridges.

■ A growing industry of cartridge re-chargers (or 're-manufacturers') has emerged to refill cartridges. Currently about 200 re-chargers refill 100,000 cartridges (although only about 30 have their own re-manufacturing capability).

■ Re-chargers disassemble the cartridge or ribbon casing, inspect it, replace worn or broken parts, and clean everything. Then the cartridge is refilled or the ribbon replaced.

Simple Things to Do

Find a Re-charger

■ Look for a re-charger in your area. Check a local computer magazine, or the Yellow Pages under 'Computer Consumables'.

■ If you can't find a re-charging service in your area, or want to check a company's reputation, contact the UK Cartridge Recycling Association (UKCRA).

NEVER ARGUE WITH HER
WHILE SHE'S CHANGING
THE TONER!

Collect Empty Cartridges and Ribbons

■ Make sure there are enough around so you'll have some to use while others are being re-charged.

■ Even if you don't re-charge, some re-chargers will take your empty cartridges and in exchange donate money to environmental groups. Con-Serv Supplies Ltd will buy one acre of endangered tropical forest in Belize for every 30 empty toner cartridges returned.

The Bottom Line

For Your Company

✍ A re-manufactured toner cartridge costs about half that of a new one.

✐ Bonus: many re-chargers provide free pick-up, delivery and unconditional guarantees on re-manufactured cartridges.

✐ Ribbons can generally be reloaded at about 40% the price of a new one. The savings are greatest for companies doing high-volume printing with mini or mainframe computers.

For the Earth

✐ Besides saving landfill space, re-charging also saves oil (the plastic used in cartridges contains about a pint of oil). Recycling cartridges in the UK could save 140,000 gallons of oil a year.

Resource

■ UK Cartridge Recycling Association (UKCRA), P.O. Box 6, Risley, Reading RG7 1YX. *Establish standards for re-chargers and can provide a list of qualified re-manufacturers in the UK.*

11 The Best Laid Plants

A study by NASA found that plants can remove up to 87% of toxic indoor air within 24 hours.

It is estimated that nearly a third of all new office buildings have indoor air quality problems. Everything from the copier to the carpet can give off hazardous gases.

A study in 1987 found that 80% of office workers experienced symptoms such as lethargy, stuffy noses, dry throats, headaches, irritated eyes and difficulty in breathing. This is known as Sick Building Syndrome (SBS), the symptoms of which disappear soon after leaving the affected building. One simple way you can improve the air quality in your office is to bring in some plants.

A Growing Concern

- Since the oil crisis in the early 1970s buildings have been designed to minimise heat losses/gains by allowing only a small amount of air to be exchanged with fresh air. Pollutants in the air are therefore re-circulated around the building, causing many of the symptoms of SBS.

- Common office pollutants include: formaldehyde (given off by particle board, wall panelling, plywood, furniture and carpeting); trichloroethylene (from some inks, paints and varnishes); benzene (from tobacco smoke, some plastics, inks and oils).

- The good news is, plants can absorb these pollutants through their leaves, roots and accompanying micro-organisms. They then convert the pollutants into food, the same process nature uses to clean air outside.

Simple Things to Do

- Put air-cleaning plants in your workplace—even on the factory floor. At least one four-to-five foot plant per 100 square feet is recommended.

- Even more effective—install a planter incorporating a fan which draws air through the soil and over a layer of charcoal.

- Some of the most effective plants are: philodendrons, parlour palms, Chinese fern, English ivy, peace lily and mother-in-law's tongue—these plants can grow under fluorescent lights, as well as in front of windows. If you have more light, spider plants and flowering plants like chrysanthemums and azaleas work well.

Success Stories

✔ Compaq Computer Manufacturing Ltd, in Scotland, have installed large trees and plants throughout their facility. The plants provide better air quality and are also good for baffling sound instead of using partitioning. 'Plants in the manufacturing area take away the factory feel and produce an environment pleasant for people to work in' says Cecilia Friel from the PR department.

✔ At Independent Insurance, Sale, 'Clean-Air' planters were installed in 1990 following a large number of complaints from staff about the poor air quality. Air quality is now appreciably better and complaints have stopped.

The Bottom Line

For Your Company

- Indoor air pollution can cost your company a lot of money. According to the Department of Employment almost 3 $1/2$ million work days were lost due to sickness in just one three-month period in 1992.

- It costs about £9,000 to put 50 'Clean-Air' planters into a 100,000-square foot office building occupied by 600 workers. Assuming the planters are operated for 10 hours a day, electricity would cost about £200 a year. If absenteeism dropped by just 5%, the company could save over £7,000 in increased productivity in the first year. Nationwide this figure could be as much as £650 million.

- Plants not only clean air, they help to create a more pleasant environment, cut noise and improve humidity levels in an air-conditioned office. These factors can raise morale, commitment and productivity.

For the Earth

- When we rely on 'natural' solutions to address pollution problems, 'we don't deplete energy or other resources that would be needed for the "higher tech" approach'—the Foliage for Clean Air Council

Resources

- The British Association of Landscape Industries (BALI), Landscape House, Henry Street, Keighley, West Yorks BD21 3DR. 0535 606139.

- Association of Interior Landscaping Contractors, 386 London Road, Mitchum, Surrey CR4 4EA. 081 640 1727.
    Both associations can put you in contact with approved local contractors.

- Clean-Air Plant Systems Ltd, Burford Lane, Lymm, Cheshire WA13 0SH. 0925 756328. Install 'Clean-Air' units to combat air quality problems.

12 Supplies and Demands

'If we're talking green, we've got to prove that we're green and the products we are using are environmentally sound.'
—The Lane Group

You're doing your part at work to try to protect the environment—but your suppliers don't seem to care. What can you do? Maybe it's time to use some of your 'customer clout' to encourage them to change their policies.

Money Talks

■ In 1992, B & Q revealed a new policy at a conference for 200 of their suppliers. It had been decided that suppliers would now be required to create and implement an environmental policy supported by a thorough environmental audit. B & Q reserved the right to review this policy and performance and to 'de-list' those who failed to show any commitment to change.

Simple Things to Do

■ Set up criteria for your suppliers, but don't ask them to do anything that your company isn't already doing. For example, you might decide you won't accept packages containing polystyrene foam 'beads'.

■ Put your policy in writing and send it to the head of each company that would be affected by the policy.

■ Be sure to apply rules uniformly. If you demand something of one company, you should demand the same thing of everyone else.

The Bottom Line

✐ Making demands of suppliers probably won't cost anything, but it sends a message that you're committed to changing the way British companies do business—and to using your influence to protect the Earth.

13 A Green Catalogue

Given the choice 60% of Britons would buy products they perceived to be less damaging to the environment.

Here's an easy way to encourage people in your company to buy environmentally sound supplies: put together your own catalogue.

Simple Things to Do

- Put together a 'catalogue' of eco-products your company can use. It doesn't have to be fancy, just type it onto a few pieces of paper (both sides, of course).

- Items to include: recycled paper goods; greener office supplies; durable products; 'green' cleaners; recycling bins. If it fits your company's needs, include energy-efficient lighting, packing materials and even computers.

- List items by category, include the product number, distributor's name, address, telephone number and any additional ordering information.

- If possible, include a letter from a company VIP requesting that buyers make an effort to purchase these products.

- Your company's buying power can help make environmentally sound products affordable—and encourage manufacturers to make a wider variety of them.

Success Stories

✔ Bodyshop International have mandated a formal purchasing policy and have produced an environmental checklist which buyers use, covering anything from computers to company cars; paper to plastic packaging. This 'green' checklist, which runs to 26 pages, has been extremely successful in consolidating and expanding the company's already wide range of environmentally preferred materials.

✔ The Lane Group don't have a formal catalogue but all contracts coming up for renewal are now subject to 'supplier discrimination'—greener products bought in have increased by 25% in a matter of months.

The Bodyshop have built the first purpose-built company creche in the UK

British Airways collect old blankets, aircraft seatcovers, headrest covers and linen from their aircraft for recycling as rags

Heathrow Airport Ltd planted 4,000 trees and shrubs and over $1/4$ of a million bulbs in 1990

JT Design Build have fitted anti-glare screens to all word processors and offered the choice of green or amber screens—excluding the use of white on black screens

Lane Group plc bought their clients rainforest adoption certificates for Christmas and got the kids from a local special school to design them

14 Invest in the Earth

In 1992 employee pension funds controlled around 30% of all the corporate stock in the UK.

Investment portfolios—including employee pension funds, the extra capital your company may keep in reserve, and your own personal investments—have tremendous power to help the Earth. How? By supporting companies with good environmental records.

Money Talks

- The total value of outstanding stock in UK corporations is about £625 billion. Pension funds hold about £185 billion of that.

- It is estimated that investments of £10 billion are now ethically screened in the UK.

- $^2/_3$ of fund managers believe that environmental issues are a significant factor for British businesses.

- Examples of ethical pension funds include The Bristol Energy Centre and The British Trust for Conservation Volunteers. Hundreds of others have a proportion of their funds ethically screened.

Simple Things to Do

Add the Environment to Your Pension Portfolio

- It is simple to add 'green' investments, provided there is sufficient interest among employees.

- The pension administrator will need a prospectus and annual report to determine any investment's potential.

Ask Your Employer to Consider Eco-investing

- ·Does your company invest its nonworking capital into a money market or mutual fund that helps the environment?

Read the company's annual report for information. This is usually listed on the balance sheet as 'Other investments' or 'Securities'. If you work for a public limited company, the information should be readily available. If you have problems, check with the firm's financial director.

■ Be determined, but tactful. Most companies don't like giving out this kind of financial information, especially to employees.

The Bottom Line

For Your Company

✍ All financial investments have a risk factor. There is no hard evidence to suggest that these environmental funds are any more successful than any other well-managed ones. On the other hand, environmental regulations are getting more stringent all the time. Companies that prevent pollution will, over the long term, be better investments than companies that wait until costly clean-ups are required.

For the Earth

✍ By investing in environmentally responsible companies, you're using your voice—along with millions of others—to support companies that are helping the Earth.

Resources

■ Commercial Union Environmental Trust, Level 1, 155 Bishopsgate, London EC2M 3YQ. 071 283 7500.

■ Clerical Medical Evergreen Fund, Narrow Plain, Bristol BS2 0JH. 0800 373393.

■ Friends Provident Stewardship Fund, UK House, 72–122 Castle Street, Salisbury, Wilts SP1 3SH. 0722 413366.

■ Merlin Jupiter Unit Trust Managers Ltd, Knightsbridge House, 197 Knightsbridge, London SW7 1RB. 071 581 8015.

■ Ethical Investment Research Information Centre (EIRIS), 504 Bondway Business Centre, 71 Bondway, London SW8 1SQ. 071 735 1351.

- Pensions and Investment Research Consultants (PIRC), Challenor House, 19–21 Clerkenwell Close, London EC1R 0AA. 071 972 9060.

- Holden-Meehan—Independent Financial Advisors, 55–57 High Holborn, London WC1V 6DX. 071 404 6442.

Remploy 'Expect our suppliers to demonstrate an environmental commitment, consistent with our own, and to co-operate with us in meeting environmental objectives'

Sainsbury's use heat extracted from refrigeration plants to warm stores and water—so no new Sainsbury's supermarket needs a boiler

Tesco was awarded five stars—the highest rating by 'The Green Consumer Supermarket Shopping Guide'

Tesco believes its energy efficiency measures to be equivalent to 1,000 tons of coal a year

BT estimate they can recycle 17,500 toner cartridges a year

15 Reflect On It

The 'typical' company has more fluorescent lights than employees.

Are you trying to conserve energy at work? Here's a simple way to save on lighting costs.

Reflections

- About half the light from a fluorescent tube is absorbed by the inside of the fitting.

- Reflectors redirect that 'lost' light. The result: you can remove half the bulbs and ballasts and still get the same amount of light.

Simple Things to Do

- Have reflectors installed in overhead fluorescent fixtures. Some companies will do an initial test area to make sure that you are happy with the results.

- Experts suggest that you install electronic ballasts and new bulbs at the same time you put in reflectors. That provides maximum savings and allows you to do everything in one operation.

The Bottom Line

For Your Company

- Converting from a twin 5-foot fluorescent luminaire with switchstart gear and T12 lamps to a single lamp with reflector, high frequency ballast and T8 lamps will cost about £65 per fixture. Each saves about £25 a year in reduced energy costs and lower maintenance. So the investment could pay for itself in about two and a half years.

For the Earth

✎ If all fluorescent lighting fixtures in British businesses used reflectors, we could save up to 10 billion kilowatt hours of electricity.

Resource

■ The Berkeley Invicta Group, Silverlight Division, Maidstone Road, Matfield, Tonbridge, Kent TW12 7JN. 0892 722202. *They make the high specular reflector.*

BT are saving 270 tons of paper a year—by using a slightly lighter-weight photocopier paper

Botley Park Hotel and Country Club was the first hotel in the UK to have an environmental (green) audit

At IBM employees are now encouraged to 'buy down' when purchasing company cars. A smaller c-c car is compensated by a cash incentive

IBM's computers don't come in white boxes anymore because the cardboard has been recycled

Bass have pledged £100,000 over three years to help save wildlife sites

16 On the Road

A single company car driven 1,000 miles a month can pump six tons of carbon dioxide into the atmosphere every year.

't's not my car, why should I worry about fuel efficiency?' That's the attitude many of us have when we're behind the wheel of a company car or one leased for a business trip. But, no matter who owns the car, the impact on the Earth is the same. By following a few basic guidelines, you will not only cut down on pollution but also save money for your company. This can translate into higher profits, bigger pay-rises and happier bosses.

Maybe you will even pick up a few tips to use on your own car.

You Auto Know

- A car gets as much as 20% better fuel mileage at 55 mph than at 70 mph.

- Driving with improperly inflated tyres can increase fuel consumption by as much as 5%.

- Experts say that driving smoothly—accelerating and slowing down gently—can increase fuel mileage by about 5%.

The Bottom Line

For Your Company

- It is possible to improve fuel mileage by as much as 20% just by driving sensibly. For a company owning 10 vehicles, that could mean fuel savings of £1,500 a year.

- Switching to smaller cars or vans for fleet use lowers vehicle purchase and fuel costs.

For the Earth

✎ If all company cars improved their fuel economy by just one mile per gallon, a saving of 500 million gallons of petrol could be made—enough to drive a 1.3 litre car around the Earth over 25,000 times.

Resource

■ 'A Guide to Environmental Best Practice for Company Transport'. Available free of charge from: Department of the Environment, P.O. Box 135, Bradford, West Yorks BD9 4HH.

17 Give Green Gifts

For the price of a bottle of Malt whisky you can adopt an acre of endangered rain forest.

Nearly every company gives gifts—to employees, customers... even the postman.

Typical gifts are diaries, pens, clocks, calenders, etc. While many of these gifts are useful, why not spend the money on something of more benefit to everyone?

Give Till it Helps

- For the cost of a desk diary you could help to buy and manage land as a nature reserve. Some examples are moorland in the Shetlands, heathland in Dorset or ancient woodlands all over the UK.

- For less than the cost of a pen set you could adopt a swan, flamingo, goose or duck through the Wildfowl and Wetlands Trust.

- For the price of two golf umbrellas you can 'buy' an acre of rainforest in the Rio Bravo area of Belize to be managed for conservation.

Simple Things to Do

- If your company already gives gifts on a regular basis, find out if management is willing to substitute comparable items that can benefit the environment.

- This isn't limited to making donations to environmental causes. You can still give gifts—for example, instead of a pen set or desk accessory, why not give a desktop recycling container or a battery re-charger? Traidcraft offer a wide range of coffees from third world sources and the Green Catalogue includes everything from low-energy desk lights to bags made from recycled tyres.

- Consider giving copies of this or other environmental books. Or make a donation in customers' or employees' names to an environmental organisation or a rainforest preservation project.

The Bottom Line

For Your Company

✍ You will be making a statement that your company is concerned about the environment.

For the Earth

✍ Whatever issue you choose to invest in—recycling, the rainforest, wildlife preservation, etc.—your money will make a difference.

✍ Bonus: environmentally responsible gifts set an example for other companies, and help make everyone aware of environmental issues.

Resources

- Programme for Belize, P.O. Box 99, Saxmundham, Suffolk IP17 2LB. 072 877501. *Buy an acre of rainforest in the Rio Bravo area of Belize. Through 'gift aid' any donation of £250 or more will increase by $^1/_3$ at no cost to yourself or PFB. Donors are provided with a certificate for each acre purchased (£25/acre).*

- World Wide Fund for Nature (WWF) UK, Panda House, Godalming, Surrey GU7 1XR. 0483 426444. *Sponsor an acre of rainforest for £20 or write for their gift catalogue.*

- Royal Society for the Protection of Birds, The Lodge, Sandy, Beds SG19 2DL. 0767 680551. *The RSPB will tailor a 'gift' to your company's requirements giving certificates and literature on your help to manage wetlands, woodlands, moorlands or mountain areas in the UK.*

- The Wildfowl and Wetlands Trust, Slimbridge, Gloucester GL2 7BT. 0453 890333. *Through them you can adopt various wildfowl.*

- Traidcraft plc, Kingsway, Gateshead NE11 0NE. 091 491 0591.

- The Green Catalogue, Freepost (BS 7348) Axbridge, Somerset BS26 2BR. 0934 732469.

- World of Difference, London Ecology Centre, 21 Endell Street, London WC2H 9BJ. 071 379 8208.

18 Don't Be a Drip

UK office workers use enough water every day to fill 150 Olympic-sized swimming pools.

The tap in the toilets has been leaking for over a year, but no one ever seems to do anything about it. That 'little leak' is not only wasting water but is also costing your company money.

The fact is, taps can waste water even when they're not leaking. According to one source, the average tap puts out as much as 6 gallons of water per minute—much more than most people need. There are simple solutions—maintenance and devices like tap regulators.

Liquid Assets

- A small drip from a worn washer can waste over 15,000 gallons of water a year—if it's a hot tap you'll be paying to heat the water.

- Depending on water pressure, it's easy to use several gallons of water just washing your hands and face.

- By installing a simple device called a tap regulator, you can cut the water flow by 30%.

- Another possibility is to install 'pressmiser' or percussive taps. These will cut the flow considerably by making the user put pressure on the tap to receive water.

- Both devices will also indirectly save energy by reducing the wastage of hot water.

Simple Things to Do

Check Your Taps

- Conduct a water audit and find out which taps are leaking and/or need regulators.

- Your maintenance department may be able to help, or you can organise people on every floor to do the survey.

Cut the Flow

- Report dripping taps to the building manager or landlord. In many cases, all it takes to repair a tap is to fit a new washer or tighten a fitting.

- Install regulators on all taps that need them. They cost very little and can be fitted in a few minutes.

- If people often leave the water running, percussive taps will solve the problem.

- If you are installing new equipment ask your plumbing contractor to install tap regulators where appropriate.

Success Story

✔ Through a variety of measures, Oxfordshire County Council have cut their water bill by over £260,000. The use of tap regulators in most of the 300 schools in the county is estimated to have saved about 6 million gallons of water in 1991/92.

The Bottom Line

✍ It is estimated that a 100-employee company uses an average of 55,000 gallons of water each year from taps alone. By installing tap regulators up to 15,000 gallons of water could be saved annually—enough to pay for the investment in under a year.

For the Earth

✍ If only 1,000 businesses with 100 employees installed tap regulators, Britain could save 15 million gallons of water a year.

Resource

- Flow Control Water Conservation Ltd, NatWest Bank Buildings, 89 Brighton Street, Wallasey, Merseyside L44 6QJ. 051 638 8811. *This company sells tap regulators and other water-saving devices*.

19 The Amazing Fluorescents

When Sterling Organics switched to compact fluorescents in their staff restaurant they cut lighting and maintenance costs by over 70%.

Everyone knows about fluorescent lights—those long, flickering tubes that give people headaches at work. Businesses have used them for many years because they give off a lot of light and use a relatively small amount of energy.

But here's something new: lighting companies now manufacture fluorescent bulbs that look and act like standard incandescents. They screw into normal fixtures, give off a pleasant light, and come on instantly, without flickering.

There's one way they're still different, though—they use only about $1/4$ of the energy of incandescents, and last about 10 times longer.

Have you seen the light?

Fluorescent Facts

- It takes eight incandescent bulbs to last the same 8,000 hours as an equivalent compact fluorescent.

- One benefit for businesses—you save on maintenance costs.

- In addition to standard overhead lights, compact fluorescents are now available as reading lights, floodlights and spotlights.

- They can be used in virtually all fixtures but are still not compatible with sophisticated dimmer systems.

Simple Things to Do

- Check with a lighting consultant or contractor to find out which of your lighting needs can be handled by compact fluorescents.

- Let employees experiment with them to see where they work best.

- There are new compact fluorescents being introduced all the time; ask contractors to keep you informed.

Success Story

✔ Edinburgh University Halls of Residence changed 740 conventional light fittings (100-watt bulbs) to 16-watt compact fluorescent lamps. In the first year, savings of £17,000 were made, paying for the new equipment in only nine months and saving 283 tons of CO_2 from being emitted.

The Bottom Line

For Your Company

✐ The initial cost of a compact fluorescent is higher than you're used to paying, £6–£14 per bulb, but you'll save money in the long run. Over its lifetime a compact fluorescent uses about £10 worth of electricity; during the same period, equivalent incandescents consume about £35 worth of electricity. So you can save up to £25 per bulb—which is like earning a minimum of 75% interest on your investment.

For the Earth

✍ Substituting a compact fluorescent for a traditional bulb could, over the life of the bulb, save the energy equivalent of about one barrel of oil or 700 pounds of coal, and eliminate the production of one ton of carbon dioxide (the major greenhouse gas) and 14 pounds of sulphur dioxide (which contributes to acid rain). By using fewer bulbs, you also cut waste.

Resource

■ The Lighting Industry Federation Ltd, Swan House, 207 Balham High Road, London SW17 7BQ. 081-675-5432. *They can refer you to manufacturers of compact fluorescents. They also produce the 'Energy Managers' Lighting Handbook'.*

20 Turn It Off

Inefficient use of office machines costs British businesses up to £400 million in electricity every year.

Is your copier on right now? How about your computer and printer?

How much energy do you think they're using?

Here's surprising news: by turning office equipment off when you're not using it, you can save up to 90% of the energy it currently consumes. In a few years, that could be enough to pay for the equipment itself.

A Switch in Time

- Up to 70% of computers and related equipment are left on all the time—even though they're used infrequently.

- According to the Rocky Mountain Institute, you could save enough electricity by turning off a standard PC monitor and printer at night and over weekends to pay for the entire purchase price of the computer within a few years.

- Because of the heat needed to fuse images onto paper, laser printers and photocopiers are especially big energy users. Keeping them warmed up takes a lot of electricity, too.

- Some equipment uses much less energy than others. For example, ink jet printers use 99% less energy than laser printers while printing, and 87% less energy when on standby. Laptop computers use as little as 1% of the typical desktop PC.

Simple Things to Do

- Turn off computers if they won't be used for at least 15 minutes. It doesn't hurt hard drives to turn them on and off. PCs that do this automatically are now on the market.

- At least, turn off the computer screens, even if only for a few minutes.

- Select a PC that uses less power. Computers are now available that consume as little as 20% of the average PC's energy. Bonus: as they don't need a fan they're also a lot quieter.

- Use laptop or notebook computers instead of desktop models whenever possible.

- Turn off printers and copiers when not in use. Most copiers have an energy-saving switch that puts the machine on 'stand-by'.

The Bottom Line

For Your Company

- Turning off just 10 monitors when they're not being used could save you £200 a year in energy costs.

- Because most office machines generate heat while they're on, turning them off reduces the demand on the air-conditioning system.

For the Earth

- Careful attention to efficiency and operation of office equipment could save energy equal to the output of a large modern power station and reduce CO_2 emissions by 5 million tons every year.

Resources

■ Energy Consumption Guide 35, 'Energy Efficiency in Offices—Small Power Loads'. Available from: Enquiries Bureau, Building Research Energy Conservation Support Unit (BRECSU), Building Research Establishment, Garston, Watford WD2 7JR. 0923 664258.

■ The Personal Systems Enquiry Centre, IBM UK Ltd, P.O. Box 32, Alencon House, Alencon Link, Basingstoke, Hants RG21 1EJ. 0256 841818. *For information on the 'Energy Saver' PC.*

21 Start a Green Team

There is no ideal size for a Green Team. It can be 30–40 people. . . or just two.

All business projects need people to provide supervision and insure follow-through.

Your environmental projects are no different. If you're serious about your company's commitment to protecting the Earth, you'll need people in charge of the effort—that's your 'Green Team'.

They're invaluable. If you're starting a recycling programme, the Green Team can find the best company to pick up recyclables—and make sure the collection runs smoothly. If you want to switch to environmentally responsible packing materials, the Green Team can research and implement the change. If employees have questions about new eco-policies, the Green Team can act as a liaison between management and workers.

Who's on the Team?

■ Volunteers are best. But some companies have successfully 'drafted' Green Team members by assigning them the responsibility, and making it part of their job description.

■ The most effective teams represent a cross-section of the company—different departments, levels and facilities. The goal is to make sure everyone in the company has access to at least one Green Team member.

■ It's a good idea to include someone from the company's top management. This demonstrates the organisation's commitment to achieving stated environmental goals, and guarantees that the group will have an advocate at high levels. Team members need to know they have a mandate to pursue eco-policies.

■ Who's in charge? There's no rule. In some companies, the senior employee runs the group's meetings; in others, a chairperson is elected. Some groups have rotating leadership systems so each member gets a crack at directing the group's efforts.

Getting Started

■ Once the members have been selected, an organisational meeting should be called.

■ Pick a chairperson. If there's no obvious choice, ask someone to volunteer.

■ Set a few reasonable goals for what the company hopes to accomplish. The first order of business, for example, might be an environmental audit so priorities can be set. Or you may have already decided you want to start a recycling programme.

■ Don't be reluctant to start small with specific issues like encouraging people to turn off equipment when it's not in use, or setting up a system for reducing paper waste when photocopying.

■ The key to making the effort work is to be as specific as possible about what you hope to accomplish.

Going Public

■ When the Green Team is organised, the rest of the company should be involved.

■ Be ready for some complaints; not everyone will be sympathetic to your effort. In fact, a few people may actually be hostile towards it.

■ If you have the blessing of top management, think about arranging a company-wide meeting at which the Green Teams are introduced. Give people a chance to ask questions, make sure employees know what's expected of them and how they can use the Green Team to help accomplish environmental goals.

■ The next best method to introduce the team is to send a memo (on recycled paper, of course) to all employees, followed up with a series of small meetings.

■ Communication is the key to making your environmental efforts work—the Green Team members are the communication links. If you're recycling, for example, and there aren't enough collection bins, or they aren't emptied often enough, employees must have a way to let management know—that's where the Green Team comes in.

■ The Green Team should give feedback to employees too, with posters, newsletters, etc. How is the company doing? People want to know they're making a difference—are there tips one department can share with another? That's part of the job.

Success Stories

✔ In Leicester, Fisher Rosemount Systems, who make process control equipment, put together a 'Green Team' in 1989. Made up of both managers and employees, the team forms an action plan each year. So far they have cut the number of landfill trips in half, phased out the use of CFCs and have achieved their target of a 90% reduction in waste generated.

Money from recycling has previously been spent on the purchase of guide dogs and is now being channelled into their energy efficiency campaign.

✔ In order to assist the implementation of their environmental policy, British Airways have introduced a number of schemes to gain input from their employees. Working groups meet on an 'as required' basis to discuss such topics as waste management, recycling, emissions and noise.

Environmental Champions, of which there are now over 200, exist to promote environmental activity and to improve their own department's environmental performance.

In addition, BA have introduced 'Greenwaves', a scheme which encourages staff to submit well-thought-out ideas for saving water, energy and other materials. One idea, to install an electronic valve to control the water supply cooling a degreasing plant, led to savings of 800,000 gallons of water a year. Initiatives on paper and aluminium recycling and the re-use of envelopes have also met with success.

The Bottom Line

For Your Company

✍ A Green Team won't cost anything extra, but it will help you to achieve your environmental goals, improving your business' image—inside and outside the company.

For the Earth

✍ Anything you can do to recycle successfully, cut down on material use, improve efficiency, etc. is good for the planet.

Renlon Group plc have reduced toxic waste by 66% since 1990

The World Wide Fund for Nature compost food residues at their HQ to use on their gardens

For every recycled carrier bag you re-use, Sainsbury's donate 1p to charity

At one of their sites, Exel Logistics saved £1,600 in 1990/91 by reducing waste disposal costs and selling materials for recycling

Exel Logistics have set a target for recycling at one of their depots— 100%

22 On Your Bike

Most journeys in the UK are a strictly local affair. $^1/_3$ are one mile or less and $^3/_4$, five miles or less—an easy cycling distance.

You're sitting in your car, firmly stuck in the usual early morning rush-hour jam. Phew!—Those fumes are lethal—it's time to wind up the window and wait.

In your off-side mirror you see a cyclist coming up fast and then disappearing into the distance. Maybe it's time to put that mountain-bike you've used twice since last Christmas to some real use.

Did You Know?

- There are 15 million bicycles in the UK, of which 6 million are in regular use.

- 1.1 million people cycle to work every day— about $4^1/_2$% of the working population.

- Sales of new bikes have consistently outstripped sales of new cars. Between 1986 and 1991, 12 million cycles were sold.

- Between 1991 and 1994 government spending on roads will amount to some £12 billion, but government spending on cycle routes has failed to materialise despite the production of an enthusiastically received blueprint in 1982.

- 99% of men and 87% of women over the age of 15 can cycle.

Simple Things to Do

- Provide showers and lockers for staff who travel to work by bicycle. A major deterrent to would-be cyclists is the lack of facilities to wash and change after a bracing ride and lack of space to store shirts, shorts and accessories.

- Make sure there is secure parking for cycles. You can park 10 bikes in the space needed for one car.

- Offer financial incentives for staff either through subsidies or interest-free loans for bicycle purchases. Some of the big manufacturers are worth approaching for bulk orders.

  Alternatively, offer bike-riders mileage allowances in the same way you do for car drivers. In Europe it's not unusual for cyclists to get a better mileage rate.

- Even better—offer a 'company bike' plus a cash sum as an alternative to a company car. Recent changes in VAT rules make it easier to do this.

- Set up a 'bike-pool' for employees to use on short trips they may make in work time.

- If you use couriers, look at cycles as an alternative. In some cities like Edinburgh, London, Manchester, Newcastle and Aberdeen firms exist to provide a cost-effective, environmentally friendly service.

Success Stories

✔ Bodyshop International have had two bike schemes in the last few years to offer employees and their families throughout the UK the chance to buy bikes at a subsidised rate. The scheme, in conjunction with Raleigh, offered a choice of four models at 60% off the normal price, as well as the option of making easy payments over 12 months. Hundreds of employees took advantage of the offer. At their Littlehampton HQ, an infrastructure which includes bike sheds and showers has resulted in about 15% of staff regularly cycling to work.

✔ Sutton Borough Council have set up an initiative called 'Borrow a Bike'—a bike pool for workers going about on council business.

  They also offer low-interest loans for periods of up to three years to enable employees to purchase bikes, and offer a mileage allowance equivalent to that of a small car.

The Bottom Line

For Your Company

🖋 Encouraging staff to cycle probably won't result in any 'above the line' saving for your company and may involve some outlay—for example, shower facilities and secure parking—but you may benefit in other ways, by gaining a fitter, more productive employee.

For the Earth

🖋 Cycling is non-polluting and doesn't require fossil fuel. A bike travels 1,600 miles on the energy equivalent of one gallon of petrol, and the energy source—food—is renewable.

🖋 If just 1% of people driving to work swapped to cycles we could save 400,000 tons of CO_2, the major greenhouse gas, from being emitted every year and take 140,000 cars off the road every day.

Resources

🖋 The London Cycling Campaign, 3 Stamford Street, London SE1 9NT. 071 928 7220. *Provide an employers' guide to supporting cycling and a corporate membership scheme.*

🖋 The Environmental Transport Association, The Old Post House, Heath Road, Weybridge, Surrey KY13 8BR. 0932 828882. *Offer a cycle insurance policy and cycle recovery scheme for members.*

23 Flushed with Success

British businesses flush more than 100 million gallons of fresh water down the toilet every day.

Most toilets use an average of two gallons of water every time they are flushed. In the 'gents', the cistern of a urinal typically flushes 24 hours a day, 365 days a year. Together, this can account for as much as 70% of all the water used in some businesses!

Simple conservation devices and new types of toilets are available, and they can cut up to 75% of the water used for each flush.

Saving water is good business—take the plunge.

Getting a Handle on the Situation

■ A simple device called a WC dam can save half a gallon—or more—per flush, by controlling the volume of water in the cistern.

■ An infra-red 'presence detector', normally located on the ceiling, will control your urinal cistern, only flushing when the urinal is used.

■ One leaky toilet can waste more than 50 gallons of water per day—that's 18,000 gallons a year.

Simple Things to Do

■ Conduct a 'toilet audit' to see which ones are leaking and which ones could benefit from water conservation devices.

■ Identify leaky toilets. Put a few drops of food colouring in the cistern. Wait about 20 minutes (make sure no one uses the toilet during this period). If coloured water escapes into the toilet bowl, you have a leak.

■ Install 'presence detectors', they're available from suppliers throughout the UK.

- Install WC dams. They're also widely available and come in kit form so you can fit them yourself in a few minutes. Alternatively, do it yourself with a sealed plastic bag of water.

- Installing new toilets? Twin-flush models use as little as 1.1 gallons per flush.

Success Story

✔ The Land Registry has had infra-red detectors fitted at most of its offices. At one location in Weymouth the £700 investment was recovered in under four months through water savings. 'They have been absolutely tremendous' says Ian Lloyd, energy manager, 'at one office we have cut our water consumption by 80%.'

The Bottom Line

For Your Company

✍ Saving water with each flush takes little effort and costs very little. In most cases you'll see a payoff in 12–18 months. BT have fitted infra-red controls in about 2,000 buildings in England and Wales and confidently expect to save 250 million gallons a year.

Resource

- Washroom Environmental, Ecology House, Park Road Industrial Estate, Park Road, Swanley, Kent BR8 8AH. 0322 614614. *Offer 'System 2000, which includes infra-red detectors and WC dams.*

24 Set Up a Recycling Programme

Hampshire County Council recovers more than four tons of office paper from 3000 workers at its Winchester HQ every month.

Your desk is piled high with paper again, and your waste basket is full. You can't fit one more memo into it.

It's the same thing every day. You know you could be recycling all that paper, but you're not sure how.

Fortunately, recycling at work is so easy that you and your co-workers can do it without even putting in any overtime.

Simple Things to Do

Focus on Office Paper

■ Offices usually start recycling programmes with 'white paper'—white stationery, photocopy paper, computer paper, and any forms on white paper. It's clean and has long fibres, so it brings the highest price when it's sold. That makes it worth your company's effort to recycle it, and worth a waste paper dealer's effort to pick it up from you.

■ You need to know how much paper your office generates. The rule of thumb is half a pound per day for each employee. That's 2.5 pounds a week per person.

Find a Waste Paper Dealer to Pick Up Your Paper

■ Ask your building manager for help. He or she may already be assisting other offices in your building with recycling programmes.

■ Check with your local authority. Many British cities now have recycling schemes; they can assist you in setting up a system and in finding someone to take your paper.

■ If neither of these approaches works, look in the Yellow Pages under 'Waste Paper' or 'Recycling'.

- Be sure to ask: What materials will they take? How much will they pay for each material (white paper, computer paper, newspaper, etc.)? Will they sign a long-term (i.e. one-year) contract? How often will they make pick-ups? Can they supply references?

- Does your company destroy confidential documents? That's important to know because recyclers usually can't accept shredded paper; it doesn't mix well with the rest of the paper.

- Most dealers won't agree to pick up anything less than 200 pounds, so you need to know how much waste paper you plan to recycle before contacting them.

- If you don't generate enough paper, talk to businesses in your building (or nearby) and see if they want to recycle too. By joining together, you can make it worth while for a collector to make a pick-up.

- If you still can't get a collector, you can always drop off the materials yourself at a recycling centre.

Who's Responsible?

- Recycling programmes need attention to keep running smoothly, so it's a good idea to have a recycling committee.

- Select one individual to act as a liaison among employees, management, cleaning staff and the collectors who pick up your materials.

- Every division or floor (say, every 30 employees) should have a recycling co-ordinator. These people can answer questions and check to make sure people aren't putting non-recyclables in recycling bins.

The Set-up

- The aim is simple: you want to direct paper that's been going into a rubbish bin into a recycling container instead.

- Provide a small container for each employee. This can be a simple cardboard box or a more elaborate container with separate compartments for different kinds of paper—'a Green Bin'.

- When the box is filled, each employee empties it into a larger central container—this can be a barrel, bin or box. Station one on each floor, in a hallway or near a photocopy machine (a lot of paper is discarded there).

- Don't make employees walk more than 50 feet to empty containers; if it takes too much effort, they won't do it.

- Keep it clean. The success of your programme will depend on making sure you get only what you want in the recycling bins. If they're contaminated with other material, the paper dealer won't accept them, so make sure the recycling bin doesn't look like a rubbish bin. Label the bin; if you want only white paper, make sure it says so—clearly.

- When your bins are full, they should be taken to a central storage or pick-up area. Office recycling programmes work best when they are integrated with the waste disposal system. In many offices, maintenance people simply transfer materials in the central bins to a storage area in the basement or at the loading bay.

- Everyone needs to know about the recycling programme. Post a memo before you begin, inviting everyone to a meeting. Show them how the system will work and explain what can and can't be recycled—a handout helps. Rember to let people know if it's a success.

■ Other materials. You should also be able to find someone to pick up bottles, cans, newspapers and maybe other materials if you have enough of them. Ask your paper collector if any other materials are accepted; if not, ask for a referral to a company that will take them.

The Bottom Line

✍ It's good business. Recycling programmes can save thousands of pounds. Ernst and Young saved £15,000 through recycling revenue and reduced waste disposal costs in their first year. They now recycle 22% of all their waste.

✍ It saves trees. Since office paper is high quality, it is used to make new paper; at the same time it saves money and landfill space. At Lloyds of London 'Green Bins' are placed at strategic points throughout the building. The initial investment cost about £200, two years later, about 140 tons of paper had been recycled, earning Lloyds over £2,000 and saving over 25,000 cubic feet of landfill space.

✍ It saves resources and money. Mobil Oil's offices in London have collected over 30 tons of paper in their first year of recycling, reducing waste disposal costs by £6,000, generating £500 in revenue and saving the equivalent of 136,000 gallons of water. Staff awareness is very high through publicity in the in-house newsletter and the enthusiasm of the general services team. Similar schemes are now being started in other UK offices.

Resources

■ Wastebusters Ltd, 31 Dover Street, London W1 3RA. 071 495 3828. *Will carry out a 'Green Audit' on your office.*

■ The Paper Recycling Co., The Print House, 18 Ashwin Street, London E8 3DL. 071 254 2362.

■ The Lothian and Edinburgh Environmental Partnership (LEEP), Freepost, Edinburgh EH6 0JP. 031 555 4010.

For Further Information

■ 'Paper, Paper!—An Office Guide to Recycled Paper and Paper Recycling'. Available from Waste Watch, 68 Grafton Way, London W1P 5LE. 071 383 3320 Price £8.95 (Oct. 1993).

■ Conservation Papers Ltd, 228 London Road, Reading RG6 1AM. 0734 665665. *Are operating 'EPIC', a one-stop data system for end-users giving guidance on what is the best recycled paper for your requirements.*

25 Take Credit

A 1991 Mintel poll revealed that a majority of British people were 'confused' about green claims.

If your company is doing good things for the Earth, why not tell the world about it?

Show and Tell

- In the post-1990 Earth Day frenzy, companies haphazardly threw themselves into 'green marketing'. It seemed that over night, every product became 'good for the environment'.

- Not all environmental claims are valid, and when people learn the truth it can backfire on a company.

- As a result, consumers are sceptical and some businesses are reluctant to call attention to themselves—even though they're making honest efforts to protect the planet.

- However, a recent survey revealed that about 60% of Britons had changed their buying habits to some degree because of environmental concerns. So it's worth letting people know your environmental practices.

Simple Things to Do

- Make sure you have all the facts about what your company is doing. That way you can build an 'environmental image' based on the truth, not hype.

- Work with an environmental group. By asking for information and advice, you may find potential problems before they're made public. A responsible group will work with you in confidence.

- Avoid well-worn slogans and meaningless terms. The British are suspicious of phrases like 'environmentally friendly'. Most people respond better to solid, believable messages.

- Work with all departments and top management before you begin 'blowing your own trumpet' to be sure the message will be reinforced throughout the company.

Where to Tell Your Story

- Once you know what you want to tell the public, communicate it in a variety of ways. For instance: your annual reports; product labels; advertisements; press releases; brochures; trade shows.

- Be ready to provide background material or relevant statistics to anyone who may ask.

Success Story

✔ Ecover, the green detergent firm, ran a 'recycled advertising' campaign employing 50 artists to create one-off collages, using waste materials, for sites throughout London. The interest generated from the media and general public increased awareness of the brand and the principles on which the company is based.

The Bottom Line

For Your Company

✍ 40% of UK consumers 'actively' seek out environmentally preferred products. The rapid growth of companies perceived to be 'green', such as Body Shop International, highlights the tangible benefits of communicating your environmental performance.

✍ Telling the world about your company's efforts on behalf of the environment is critical. How you back up your message is even more critical.

For the Earth

✍ By sharing your story in a positive, credible way, you set a good example for other companies to follow, as you help to educate the public about how everyone can make a difference.

Resource

■ Greenmantle Marketing and Advice Services, Thornbury House, 18 High Street, Cheltenham GL50 1DZ. 0242 255357. *An environmental marketing and public relations firm.*

The RSNC have schemes to adopt anything from a peat bog to a roadside verge

Post office counters are expecting to cut paper usage by 20% through re-use and the introduction of electronic mail

Remploy have asked their workforce, via the company newsletter, how they can best meet the aims of their environmental policy

Van den Berghs and Jurgens have put their electricity bills back five years by installing new lamp fittings and reflectors

Pilkington Glass Ltd recycles over 99% of its (pre-consumer) flat glass waste

Kyocera have introduced a 'green' printer with a drum that never needs replacing

26 Give It Away

British companies throw away enough desks and chairs each year to furnish the House of Commons a hundred times.

Your whole department just got new desks. Now what are you going to do with the old ones?

Unfortunately, there's a good chance they'll finish up in landfills.

But they don't have to. There are lots of people who can put your old office equipment to good use. All it takes is a few simple phone calls to find them.

Circular Files

- Each year British businesses buy about 100,000 desks, 500,000 chairs, 150,000 tables and 250,000 filing cabinets.

- Businesses also throw away hundreds of thousands of old or outdated machines, fixtures, supplies, computers, carpets, books and vehicles.

- Much of this equipment is in working condition, but simply isn't needed any more. However, many companies throw away the items, because they have no system in place to distribute them.

Simple Things to Do

Keep Track of Surplus

- Have an employee group (your Green Team) set up a system to handle unwanted equipment.

- Ask department heads to notify the group whenever there are usable items they don't want or need.

- Arrange for the items to be brought to a central storage area until they can be picked up.

- Don't overlook the little things. For example, old magazines can be donated to local schools, hospitals or nursing homes.

Pass It On

- Contact charities, the Salvation Army or other non-profit-making organizations. They'll usually arrange a pick-up within a few days.

- Even better, if you're unsure of whom—to contact ask the Charities Aid Foundation for their directory, 'Waste-Not', which will list charities with offices in your area.

- One organisation will use your unwanted office equipment to train 'challenged' people to re-enter the job market.

Success Stories

✔ NatWest donated second-hand office furniture and equipment to the World Wide Fund for Nature (WWF) which was shipped to WWF's headquarters in the Korup National Park in Cameroon.

✔ The London Wildlife Trust has received most of its chairs, tables, desks and filing cabinets from local businesses. The charity, which helps to conserve wildlife in London through direct projects and educational links, has also received computers for its central office.

   At one site, tree surgeons give wood chip to use on paths—a waste product they would have to pay to dispose of and the Trust would normally have to buy.

The Bottom Line

For Your Company

✎ Your company can't receive tax write-offs for donating things it might otherwise have thrown away—but it won't cost you anything more than a few phone calls.

✎ Donations can bring your company good publicity.

For the Earth

✍ If every company donated just one desk or chair it might have thrown away we could save as much as 5 million cubic feet of landfill space every year.

Resources

- ■ Action Resource Centre, 1st Floor, 102 Park Village East, London WW1 3SP. 071 383 2200. *Will match donations to charities or voluntary organisations.*

- ■ Frontline Careers Training Agency, Unit 4, Block 1, Woolwich Dockyard Industrial Estate, Church Street, Woolwich, London SE18 5PQ. 081 855 6633. *Will use office equipment to train people with difficulties. They call it 'Customised Rehabilitation'.*

27 Corporate Communications

British companies send an estimated 1 billion catalogues every year. That's enough paper to print over 500,000 copies of this book.

Communication is an intrinsic part of business. Through catalogues, brochures, packages, invoices, etc., your company is constantly in touch with customers and suppliers.

You send hundreds, thousands, maybe tens of thousands of messages every week. So why not take the opportunity to share your concerns about the environment, and pass on useful information?

Hear, Hear

■ Company newsletters reach thousands of people. One example: The 'Courier', an in-house publication of Post Office counters, is sent to about 40,000 staff and post-masters every month.

■ British Telecom send out more than 8 million telephone bills every month—100 million a year.

■ It is estimated that the average adult sees about 50 TV advertisements a day, or about a week's worth of ads a year.

Simple Things to Do

For Employees

■ Include eco-information in your company newsletter or other in-house publications. Print a regular column on the environment, or encourage employees to write in and pass on tips.

■ Arrange for speakers to visit during work or after hours to discuss the things employees can do. Environmental groups, utilities and government agencies will often send speakers at no charge.

For Customers

■ If you have a formal environmental policy, publish it in company brochures and reports.

■ Include environmental tips in your company's catalogues and brochures, etc.

■ Sponsor a 'community forum' on the environment. Invite speakers from environmental organisations to give presentations.

Success Stories

✔ Pilkington Glass Ltd have produced a 'green video' in order to undertake educational programmes and discussion on green issues for employees.

The video, which looks at subjects like pollution, recycling, transport, litter and the ozone threat through the eyes of children, was shown to all PGL employees in the UK.

This has been followed up by the distribution of Pilkington plc's corporate environmental policy to all employees and shareholders.

✔ Courtaulds produce a bi-monthly Journal, 'Environment Matters'. The aim of the publication, now in its third year, is to inform Courtaulds' employees on environmental issues and company environmental policy and to encourage readers to contribute to the improvement of the company's environmental performance.

✔ Sainsbury's produce a small booklet 'Living Today - The Environment' which advises their customers on the causes, effects and possible solutions to global warming, the destruction of the ozone layer and waste. It looks briefly at what the consumer can do and gives examples of Sainsbury's actions and policies.

The Bottom Line

For Your Company

✍ Letting employees know you're committed helps to give them a sense of purpose, and adds value to the work they do for you. It can increase motivation, morale and productivity.

✍ Educating customers helps them to appreciate your company and products.

For the Earth

✍ The more people who understand the environmental challenges we face, and what we can do about them, the better chance we have of overcoming them.

Resources

■ 'The Ethical Consumer', ECRA Publishing, 16 Nicholas Street, Manchester M1 4EJ. 061 237 1630.

■ 'The New Consumer', 52 Elswick Road, Newcastle Upon Tyne NE4 6SN. 091 272 1148.

Bi-monthly and quarterly updates respectively on environmentally responsible products.

■ 'The Universal Green Office Guide', a 48-page booklet covering green issues and office products, available from any Universal Office Supplies outlet in the UK for £1.95 (Oct. 1993 price).

28 Watt's Up

Lighting accounts for over $^1/_3$ of the energy used in commercial spaces.

It's past going home time, and you're the last one to leave the office. As you walk out of the door, you can't help but notice that nearly every overhead light is still on. Why hasn't anyone bothered to turn them off? Well, maybe the cleaners will do it—or will they?

Bright Thinking

- Half of office lighting is wasted either through inefficient bulbs, poor design or improper maintenance.

- The main reason: most light bulbs are inefficient, they give off more heat than light. With some types of bulbs, 90% of the electricity used is turned into heat, and only 10% becomes light. Many new bulbs can, however, cut energy use dramatically.

- Another reason: companies don't plan their lighting needs when they design their buildings or offices. Modern design and architectural techniques can reduce lighting costs significantly.

Simple Things to Do

- Do a lighting audit; put light where it will do the most good. Use 'occupancy sensors' in rooms that are infrequently used— toilets, storage rooms, etc. The sensors detect people in a room; when the room is empty the lights are automatically switched off.

- Replace regular spotlights with reflectorized halogen bulbs. These provide a cooler beam, white light and 50–60% energy savings. Replace floodlights with reflectorized compact fluorescents; these can cut energy use by 75–80%.

- If you use fluorescent (tube) lights: switch to T8 trichromatic bulbs. They produce the same amount of light as standard T12 lamps, but have better colour and use 10% less energy.

- Install new high-frequency electronic ballasts. Many existing fluorescents are run by switchstart gear. The 'state of the art' high frequency ballasts give up to 25% energy savings. Bonus: they don't hum or flicker like the older ones do and can last up to 50% longer. At about £20 each, they'll pay for themselves in three years.

- If you use mercury vapour lights: replace them with high-pressure sodium vapour bulbs. A 250-watt or 400-watt bulb produces more light, at lower cost, than the typical 1000-watt mercury bulb and is ideal for car parks, loading bays and other outdoor areas.

Success Story

✔ The Dover Harbour Board conducted a major overhaul of lighting needs for its main passenger terminal building. They now use smaller or fewer lamps, high-performance reflectors and more efficient ballasts in the interior lighting.

Electricity costs for the building have been cut by nearly £20,000 per year for an investment of just over £48,000, giving a payback in under $2^1/_2$ years.

In addition, maintenance costs have fallen dramatically as light is now provided by fewer bulbs with longer lives.

The Bottom Line

For Your Company

✐ Many lighting improvements can rapidly pay for themselves. Because it runs cooler, energy efficient lighting can also reduce air conditioning costs by 8–10%.

For the Earth

✐ If all businesses adopted commonly available high-efficiency lighting techniques, we could save about 5% of all the electricity used in the UK. We could also cut sulphur dioxide emissions by 4% and carbon dioxide emissions by 3%.

Resource

- The Lighting Industry Federation, Swan House, 207 Balham High Road, London SW17 7BQ. Tel: 081 765 5432. *Will put you in touch with companies providing energy-efficient lighting.*

29 Share the Wealth

Britain gave £16.1 billion in charitable gifts in 1990—3.4% of GDP.

I f you're like most people, your postbag is flooded with pleas for money from all kinds of groups. It's hard to decide who's worthy and who's not.

At thousands of workplaces, the problem has been solved by something called 'Give As You Earn'. It's simple: everyone gives a few pounds from their monthly salary and the money goes to a cross-section of well-managed charities. It quickly adds up to millions of pounds a year.

Why not use the same approach to protect our environment?

Did You Know?

■ Charitable donations are going down in real terms but 'Give As You Earn' schemes experienced an increase of almost 15% in 1992.

■ 'Give As You Earn' schemes are the most cost-effective way to raise charitable donations. About 95p of every pound goes directly to the charity. With direct-mail campaigns, only about 2% of letters get responses and only 75p of every pound may end up reaching the charity.

■ Statistics show that people will give more if they do it in small amounts over a period of time. It's easier to give £3 every pay day than write a single cheque for £50.

■ Most 'Give As You Earn' schemes now offer an environmental option.

Simple Things to Do

Set Up a Workplace Campaign for the Earth

■ First, find out if there's enough interest. Talk with employees and management. Make sure everyone understands how the programme works. Remember: it's strictly voluntary. If you've never had a 'Give As You Earn' scheme, get help from experts.

■ Most schemes begin with a campaign to sign people up. Groups like the Charities Aid Foundation can provide a directory of charities for individuals to make their elective choice. Environmental groups like Friends of the Earth, Greenpeace or the World Wide Fund for Nature will come and explain how the donations will be used.

■ Employees are given a form which authorises the salary department to deduct a certain amount from their pay, which can be donated to a charity of their choice or put into a general fund.

■ Donations are deducted at source before tax is calculated. In some workplaces employers will also pay the 5% administration fee and match some or all of the funds contributed by employees—making it possible for 200% of your donation to go directly to the nominated charity. The organiser will keep track of donations and provide information to be used at tax time.

Success Stories

✔ British Telecom match all the donations pledged by their employees and cover the administration fee. This translates into and annual pay-out of $£^3/_4$ million from 'Give As You Earn'.

✔ In 1992 the Charities Aid Foundation helped raise over £10 million from the private and public sectors.

The Bottom Line

For Your Company

✎ A 'Give As You Earn' scheme involves some costs—a few pence per donation for the typical workplace.

✎ Experts report that employee morale and motivation go up during workplace campaigns.

For the Earth

✎ Hundreds of environmental organisations provide valuable services in educating the public and mobilising action to help the Earth. By helping employees to contribute to these groups, you make it easier for these groups to accomplish their missions.

Resource

■ Charities Aid Foundation, Foundation House, Coach and Horses Passage, The Pantiles, Tunbridge Wells, Kent TN2 5TZ. Tel: 0892 512244.

30 Maintain a Green Fleet

A well-tuned company car can use as much as 10% less petrol than a poorly tuned one.

C ars and trucks are not great for the environment, but it's hard to do business without them. British businesses put millions of vehicles on the road every day.

The way your company maintains its 'fleet' — whether it consists of 1,000 vehicles or just one—can make a difference to the planet.

Parts of the Problem

- More than 22 million tyres and 2 million batteries are dumped into landfills every year. Old batteries can leak lead and sulphuric acid into groundwater supplies.

- Although much of the metal from the 1.5 million cars scrapped in the UK each year is re-processed, 500,000 tons of other materials, in the form of a black toxic sludge, go to landfills.

- Car air-conditioners are responsible for ozone destruction. How? When air-conditioners leak, lost coolant releases ozone-depleting CFCs into the atmosphere.

- 28 million gallons of motor oil go missing every year, mostly into freshwater systems. The oil from one· oil change can leave a visible film over four acres of water.

Simple Things to Do

- Computerise the maintenance schedules for all company vehicles, and make sure that they are tuned regularly. You'll improve fuel mileage, lengthen engine life and reduce the cost of running your own vehicles.

- Keep all tyres properly inflated; poorly inflated tyres can cut fuel consumption by up to 5%.

- Carefully service vehicle air-conditioners. Servicing should be undertaken once a year with a garage that has a device to capture and recycle the CFCs (this is now a legal requirement in the UK).

- Use unleaded petrol or change all your company cars to diesel—it's cleaner and cheaper.

- Patronise garages that recycle motor oil, tyres, batteries, antifreeze and other fluids. Your company's money can be a persuasive force in getting services to become more environmentally sensitive.

- Look into setting up recycling programmes if you run your own maintenance facilities. Contact your local authority or fleet supplier on how and where to dispose safely of car parts and fluids.

Success Stories

✔ In December 1992, BMW set up the UK's first disassembly and recycling centre. Brake fluid is recycled for further use, as are aluminium, plastic and glass, either for new BMWs or for other industrial and domestic uses.

✔ Sainsbury's are reducing and 'rejuicing' their company car fleet. Numbers are down 3% in the first half of 1993 and two to three now run on diesel. The average fuel consumption for the fleet is now 45 mpg.

The Bottom Line

For Your Company

✍ The cost of regular maintenance could be offset by the increased fuel efficiency and useful life-span of your vehicles. According to the RAC a poorly maintained vehicle can cost up to 35% more in running costs over its lifecycle—this can amount to thousands of pounds.

For the Earth

✒ If every company-owned vehicle improved its fuel consumption by just 10%, we could save 200 million gallons of petrol and keep nearly 3 billion pounds of CO_2 from entering the atmosphere, as well as reducing emissions of many other pollutants.

Resources

■ Environmental Transport Association (ETA), The Old Post House, Heath Road, Weybridge KT13 8RS. 0932 828882. *An environmental breakdown organisation who produce 'The ETA Car Buyer Guide' which looks at the 'greenest' cars available in the UK.*

■ RAC National Technical Centre, RAC House, Brockhurst Crescent, Walsall WS5 4Q7. 0345 345500 (Local rate calls).

■ AA, Technical Advice and Information Unit, Norfolk House, Basingstoke, Hants RG21 2EA. 0256 20123.

31 Leaf It Alone

Imagine 400 25-pound rubbish bags bulging with grass clippings. That's what just one acre of lawn yields in a year.

British businesses are always looking for ways to eliminate waste and cut costs. Here's a good one: start composting instead of paying someone to haul your green waste to an overflowing landfill.

Turf It Out

- British companies landfill about 2 million tons of green waste every year.

- In landfills, green waste doesn't get the sunlight or oxygen it needs to decompose easily. In fact, it releases methane gas, which can pollute ground water and contributes to global warming.

- But, if it's left to decompose naturally, green waste adds nutrients such as nitrogen, potassium and phosphorous to the soil.

Simple Things to Do

Start Composting

- Ask your company's landscaping service what they know about composting. Do they have the equipment needed to shred leaves and chip wood? Are they willing to learn?

- Consider setting up your own composting system. You need a small outside area and some equipment (see Resources).

- Let someone else do it. Some companies will compost your waste and sell it to gardeners.

- Call your local waste authority to see if it operates a municipal composting programme.

Rake Expectations

- ■ Let it lie. Keep grass 2–3 inches high, and trim it a little at a time. Clippings will drop between the blades of grass, helping the soil to retain moisture, prevent weeds, and fertilise the soil.

- ■ Several manufacturers sell mowers with blades that chop clippings into fine particles and blow them down into the grass roots.

Success Stories

- ✔ The North London Waste Authority have composted 20,000 tons of green organic waste in the last two years—half from commercial sources. The operation has produced about 5,000 tons of compost which is sold to a variety of sources, including landscape companies who also deliver their waste.

- ✔ The city of Dundee District Council collect up to 120 tons of botanical waste a day in summer for their multi-purpose composting facility. The authority, faced with diminishing landfill space, were in payback almost immediately with an income of £80 per ton from high quality compost.

The Bottom Line

For Your Company

✍ Shanks and McEwan are now offering composting as an alternative to landfill for clients at two sites in the UK. They say that recycling your green waste should cost less and certainly not more than landfill.

For the Earth

✍ By recycling green waste we can save landfill space. For example, in the seven boroughs of North London 60,000 tons of green waste could easily be composted each year. Bonus: composting can help to save our peat bogs, a unique and important habitat for rare plants and animals.

Resources

■ Henry Doubleday Research Association, Ryton-on-Dunsmore, Coventry CB8 3LG. 0203 303517. *An excellent information source on composting. Single membership is £14 a year (Oct. 1993 rate).*

■ The Composting Unit, Wye College, University of London, Wye, Nr. Ashford, Kent TW25 5AH. 0233 813164. *Technical consultants who will perform composting trials on particular waste streams and advise on setting up midi-scale composting.*

■ Shanks and McEwan Energy Services Ltd, The Cottage, Church Road, Woburn Sands, Milton Keynes MK17 8GA. 0908 282822.

32 Everyone into the Pool

Up to 75% of cars travelling to and from work, and stuck in traffic jams, tend to have only one occupant—the car driver!

If you're concerned about the effect of cars on the environment but can't take public transport, here's an alternative: join a car-pool or a mini-bus—and get your business to support it.

Did You Know?

- The CBI claims that delays to deliveries and hold-ups to the travelling public cost businesses as much as £5 billion a year.

- American studies have shown that people who drive in congested traffic have higher blood pressure.

- According to surveys, the main reasons people don't join a car-pool are: they want access to a car in case of a family emergency or if they have to work late; and they don't like the idea of riding with strangers.

- However, car-sharing can actually be enjoyable. The social benefits of chatting to friends and colleagues during the journey may well reduce some of the stress caused by driving.

Simple Things to Do

Car-sharing

- Set up a car-sharing programme in your company. The goal: match riders and drivers who live within a few miles of one another.

- One easy method: place a large map on a bulletin board and have employees pin their names and phone numbers to their neighbourhoods on the map.

- Make lists of the names and phone numbers of people who live near each other and distribute them to each member of the group.

- Give employees an incentive by providing free or reduced-rate parking and prime parking spaces for car-sharers.

- If your company has too few employees to organise a pool, contact other local businesses, your local authority or public library information service for news of initiatives in your area.

Mini-bus Pools

- A company can also buy or rent a mini-bus for groups of employees to use. Employees can pay for their own fuel, maintenance and insurance. And instead of hiring a driver, let an employee drive at no charge and have the use of the van at weekends.

- Paint your company name on the mini-bus and a message—'We're doing our part to reduce pollution.' You'll have a moving advertisement for your business' environmental commitment.

- Set up a 'Guaranteed Ride Home Scheme'. Offer pool members the assurance of transport home if it's needed.

Success Stories

✔ The Bodyshop International encourage car-pooling at their Littlehampton HQ. Interested parties can match up via notice-boards and a data base is now being developed. As many as 30% of the site's 600 employees now use car-sharing, taking up to 100 cars off the road every day.

✔ The World Wide Fund for Nature have put up a map in a central area. Staff put their initials and extension numbers on a pin enabling people to match up and form 'pools'. Most staff travel from London to the building in Surrey; up to 20% now reduce travel costs, both to themselves and to the environment, by car-sharing.

✔ The Leicester Ecology Trust are running a scheme called 'Leicester Share'. Individuals are provided with a registration form and specify their work schedules and preferences on smoking, gender and driving. People are matched using the second number of their post-codes. The success rate is 20% and rising. Similar schemes are working in other cities including Edinburgh and Nottingham.

The Bottom Line

For Your Company

✍ Car-sharing will cost your company very little—perhaps the price of a large local map—but will produce tangible benefits.

The more staff involved, the less cars you'll have to accommodate in that precious car park. It has also been claimed that car-sharing can build employee morale and increase their productivity by reducing stress on the journey to work.

For the Earth

✍ The average commuting car holds just 1.3 passengers. If each commuting car carried just one more person, we could save more than 4 million gallons of petrol and keep more than 60 million pounds of carbon dioxide out of the atmosphere—every day.

Resource

■ Transport 2000, Walkden House, 10 Melton Street, London NW1 2EJ. 071 388 8386. *Provides a journal, 'The Transport Report' for members.*

33 Close the Loop

If UK business recycled the 3 million tons of waste the Government suggests is viable, we could create 10,000 new and socially useful jobs.

Every week your office collects its paper, glass and cans. It makes you feel good to know all that material is being saved, but what happens to it after it leaves your business? That depends on you.

The market for recycled products, and companies producing recycled goods, will grow if your company is committed not only to saving waste but also to purchasing recycled goods.

Did You Know?

Paper isn't the only recycled product available, for example:

- Car tyres can be recycled by grinding them up and making them into carpet underlay.

- You can buy pens, pencils and rulers made partly or entirely out of recycled plastic or reclaimed wood.

- Rubbish bags made of recycled material are available—as well as recycling bins made entirely out of recycled plastic. High quality recycled paper is available for almost any use.

Simple Things to Do

- Find out if any products you purchase are made from recycled materials—there should be a symbol indicating this.

- Caution: Not all 'recycled' products contain 100% recycled material, some have only a small percentage. You may have to ask to find out the exact amount.

- Contact the manufacturer for a catalogue or product specification. If there are several products to choose from, this information may help you determine which one has the highest percentage of recycled material.

- Many companies will send a sample so you can decide for yourself whether the product will meet your standards.

- When you do purchase these products, tell others in your company. People enjoy knowing that they're contributing to saving the Earth.

The Bottom Line

For Your Company

✍ Many recycled products are competitive, but some do cost more than unrecycled ones—however, higher costs are almost always the result of a weak market. When your business—and thousands like it—begins buying recycled goods on a regular basis, the prices will drop. Someone has got to be a leader, why not you?

For the Earth

✍ Buying recycled goods saves energy and raw materials. For example: when a steel mill uses recycled scrap, it cuts related water pollution, air pollution and mining wastes by 70%. Recycling aluminium saves 95% of the energy used in making items from virgin material.

Resources

- Duralay, Broadway, Heslington, Rossendale, Lancs BB4 4LS. 0706 224915. *Manufacture carpet underlay from recycled tyres.*

- Helix Ltd, P.O. Box 15, Lye, Stourbridge, West Midlands DY9 7AJ. 0384 424441. *Produce a printed ruler with your company or conference logo from seven recycled plastic cups, and are looking to market a range of recycled products.*

- The Green Business Company, Studio One, 114 Walcot Street, Bath BA1 5BG. 0225 480556. *The UK's largest range of green office products including pens, pencils, papers, envelopes and packaging materials made from recycled materials.*

- Linpac Environmental Products, Road 1, Industrial Estate, Winsford, Cheshire CW7 3RA. 0606 593921. *Manufacture wheelbins, crates and 'blue boxes' from 95% recycled plastic for kerbside collections.*

- Easi-Bind International, Adams Close, Heanor, Derbys DE75 7XA. 0800 626411 (Freephone). *Make clip files, presentation wallets, personal organisers and other products from recycled polypropylene waste.*

- Alida Recycling Ltd, Heanor, Derbys DE7 7RG. 0773 530530. *Manufacture carrier bags from post-consumer polythene waste.*

- Glasdon UK Ltd, Freepost, Government Services Division, Preston New Road, Blackpool FY4 4BR. 0253 694621. *The 'Enviropol' range includes planters, benches, tables, pack seats and fencing made from recycled plastic.*

- Porous Pipe Ltd, P.O. Box 2, Colne, Lancs BB8 7BY. 0282 871778. *Make porous pipe which can be laid above or under the ground to water plants. Made from recycled material.*

- VMB Ltd, Blackpole Trading Estate (East), Blackpole Road, Worcester WR3 8SG. 0905 755000. *Make and sell 'envirolope' self-sealing mailing bags and envelopes made from recycled waste polythene.*

- Natural Wood Products, Mishet Park, Crucible Close, Coleford, Gloucestershire GL16 8RE. 0594 810610. *Manufacture the 'big bin', an office collection bin for recycled paper, made from recycled paper.*

- Evergreen Recycled Fashions, Albert Mills, Bradford Road, Batley Carr, Dewsbury, W. Yorks WF13 2HE. 0924 453419. *Breaks down items of clothing or other textile material and uses the fibres to make new items.*

- Scrap, Scrap Endurance Works, High Street, Coalport, Telford, Salop TF9 7HX. 0952 586754. *New items of clothing and fashion accessories are made from 'scrap'.*

- Triumph-Adler, Ipswich Road, Colchester CO4 4EJ. 0206 845251. *Use re-granulated ribbon cassettes to form a new casing for the 'cyclo' typewriter.*

- Fort Sterling Ltd, Mansell Way, Horwich, Bolton BL6 6JL. 0204 68611. *Make recycled kitchen towel, serviettes and napkins.*

- Roltech Ltd, Norman Park, Bar Hill, Cambridge CB3 8SS. 0954 780436. *Make recycled cash register and adding machine rolls.*

- Pennine Data Forms, 59 Preston New Road, Blackburn, Lancs BB2 6AY. 0254 680066. *Supply recycled computer paper.*

- Dunlop Footwear Ltd, Road 1, Winsford, Cheshire CW7 3QF. 0606 592041. *Manufacture recycled wellington boots from re-granulated PVC.*

- National Directory of Recycling Information, available from Waste Watch, 68 Grafton Way, London W1P 5LE. 071 383 3320. Price £9.95 (Oct. 1993).

34 Beat the Heat

It takes the equivalent of more than 1 million tons of coal to heat British offices every week.

Somewhere in your building, quietly (or not so quietly) working away, is a combination heater and air-conditioner. The engineers call it an HVAC system; it's a big, clunky device that rarely gets any attention. As a result, systems are often poorly maintained, or are operated incorrectly. In some cases the equipment gets old and inefficient, and nobody even notices it.

If you're willing to take a little time, there's a lot of energy and money to be saved.

Let's start with the heating system.

When You're Hot, You're Hot

- Most building heating systems have two basic parts—the boiler (which generates heat) and fans (which move the heat).

    You may be surprised to learn that the biggest energy user isn't the boiler, it's the fans. They can make up as much as half of a building's entire electricity bill.

- Experts say that regular maintenance can increase equipment life by up to 200%. On the other hand, ignoring maintenance can reduce equipment life by half. An inefficient heating system can use twice as much energy as an efficient one.

Simple Things to Do

Keep the System Tuned

- Have the entire heating system checked annually by a qualified mechanical engineer. Don't leave this important task to your building engineer, who may not have the expertise to do the job right.

- Is the fan speed adequate for your building's needs? Ask the engineer. If the fans aren't adjusted properly, the whole system runs inefficiently. A simple adjustment may cut energy costs by 20% or more.

- Clean filters regularly. You can tell the filters are dirty if there's dirt or soot around the ceiling vents. Dirty filters restrict air flow, requiring the system to work harder. Bonus: cleaning filters also improves indoor air quality.

Upgrade the System

- Install variable-speed fans. Most fans operate at a constant speed, variable-speed fans adjust themselves to deliver only the amount of air the building needs at any given moment. Installation costs are typically recouped within three years through reduced energy costs.

- If the system is over 25 years old, think about replacing the boiler. The cost of a new boiler can pay for itself in as little as one year through energy savings.

The Bottom Line

For Your Company

Keeping a heating system maintained can cost very little but can yield big savings in reduced energy costs. Experts say that most building owners can cut their heating bills by as much as half through preventive maintenance. For a 100,000-square foot building, that's an estimated saving of over £10,000 a year.

For the Earth

It's estimated that if just half of all offices used preventive maintenance techniques on their heating systems, we could save enough energy to light all the homes in the UK for six months every year.

Resources

■ Heating Ventilation Contractors Association (HVCA), Esca House, 34 Palace Court, Bayswater, London W2 4JG. 071 229 2488. *They will suggest qualified mechanics in your area— and guarantee the quality of the work.*

■ Energy Consumption Guide 19, 'Energy Efficiency In Offices'. Available free from: Enquiries Bureau, Building Research Conservation Support Unit (BRECSU), Building Research Establishment, Garston, Watford WD2 7JR. 0923 664258.

35 Cool Aid

In air-conditioned offices 30–40% of the energy bill is typically attributable to air-conditioning alone.

If you work in a typical new office building, you can't open the windows. That means when it gets hot and stuffy, your only option is to turn up the air-conditioning.

Keeping things cool at work takes a lot of money and energy— the equivalent of about 200,000 tons of coal every year in the UK. So it makes sense for your company to try to keep its costs low, as well as the temperature. The best way to do that is to make sure the air-conditioning system is well maintained.

Cold Comfort

- An inefficient cooling system can use as much as 20% more energy than a well-tuned one.

- Several thousand installed A/C systems still use ozone-destroying chlorofluorocarbons (CFCs) as a refrigerant. When the system isn't properly maintained, CFCs can leak out—anything up to a gallon a minute.

Simple Things to Do

- Have the air-conditioning system checked annually by a qualified mechanical engineer. Make sure that this includes testing the refrigerant system for leaks.

- Ask your technician to use a device to capture chlorofluorocarbons during repair and maintenance. These devices not only keep CFCs out of the atmosphere, they allow the gas to be recycled and re-used.

Reduce the Heat

- Lights and machines create heat. By turning them off when they are not in use, you can reduce a building's cooling requirements by up to 10%.

- Consider using shades and other window treatments that can keep heat out in the summer. (See page 112.)

Upgrade the System

- Consider installing a 'Variable Air Volume (VAV) System', a centralised air-conditioning system which supplies a variable volume of air of a constant temperature (and humidity) to each area of the building.

- Want a less expensive device? Try a 'Constant Volume (single zone)' system. This delivers fixed volumes of air to the different areas of a building. The air can be heated, cooled, humidified or de-humidified as appropriate.

- Both systems might deliver payback through energy savings in as little as three years.

HOW DO YOU LIKE MY IDEA FOR SAVING ON THE HEATING COSTS?

Success Story

✔ By installing a new type of air-conditioning system that creates and stores ice during off-peak hours (when rates are lower), the 90-year-old Halifax Building Society premises in Moorgate, London have cut their air-conditioning costs by a considerable amount.

The Bottom Line

For Your Company

✍ A small investment in air-conditioning maintenance can yield a big payoff. A typical 100,000-square foot building can save as much as £6,000 a year simply by keeping the system in good shape.

For the Earth

✍ If half of all business air-conditioners were maintained at peak efficiency, we could save enough energy to drive a car around the equator an estimated 50,000 times.

Resources

■ Good Practice Guide No. 71, 'Selecting Air Conditioning Systems'. Available free from: Enquiries Bureau, Building Research Energy Conservation Unit (BRECSU), Building Research Establishment, Garston, Watford WD2 7JR. 0923 664258.

■ HEVAC, Stirling House, 6 Furlong Road, Bourne End, Bucks SL8 5DG. 0628 531186. *They'll help locate a qualified contractor. Write for a free brochure, 'Refrigeration Update— Safeguarding Your Business'.*

36 CFC You Later

Less than 5% of CFCs are being reclaimed. The other 95% are either incinerated or escape into the atmosphere.

Y ou've read about the depletion of the ozone layer and you're concerned. What can you do about it?

It's not easy to attack a problem you can't see.

The ozone layer is some 6–30 miles over our heads—high enough so most of us don't even know it's there. Yet 5% of it may already be gone due to human activity, and if the trend continues, all life on Earth will be threatened.

British businesses have a special responsibility to do their part to save the ozone layer.

Four Enemies of the Ozone Layer

- CFCs. You may know that chlorofluorocarbons are destroying the ozone layer, but do you know how your business uses them? The most common way is as a coolant (most commonly R12) in air-conditioners and refrigeration systems.

- Methyl Chloroform (also called 1,1,1 trichloroethane) is weaker than CFCs, but is used in larger quantities. This is in products like correction fluid, dry cleaning sprays, leather cleaners and other aerosols—even some that say 'ozone-friendly'. Businesses use it mainly as a cleaning solvent in the fabrication of metal. It's also frequently used to fabricate adhesives and clean electronic parts.

- Carbon tetrachloride is a poisonous, non-flammable, colourless liquid typically used by chemical companies to make other chemicals.

- Halon, a potent enemy, is most often used in fire extinguishers.

Simple Things to Do

Do an 'Ozone Audit'

- Check manufacturing processes. What are you using? Look for alternatives—substitutes are available for many ozone depleters.

- Air-conditioners: have your building's cooling system checked for leaks.

- Refrigerators and freezers: if you have a kitchen facility, have the refrigerator and freezer checked.

- Fire extinguishers: buy only halon-free fire extinguishers. Halon-free will be labelled 'dry powder' or 'foam'.

- Company cars: have the air-conditioning checked.

Success Story

✔ British technology helped to create this problem, the same technology can help to control it. For instance, Refridgerant Reclaim Ltd have developed a '4-Rs' programme: recover, recycle, reclaim and re-use—one of the most comprehensive systems in the world. CFCs are captured during repair by a portable unit, processed to take out all impurities and then made available for further use. By the end of 1993 the system will have kept 200,000 pounds of CFCs out of the atmosphere.

The Bottom Line

For Your Company

✍ The same leaks that damage the ozone layer cost your company money. A properly functioning air-conditioner, for example, requires less energy.

For the Earth

✍ For every CFC molecule that's prevented from entering the atmosphere, 100,000 molecules of the ozone layer may be spared.

Resources

- ICI Chemicals and Polymers Ltd, P.O. Box 13, The Heath, Runcorn, Cheshire WA2 4QF. 0928 511708. *Manufacture KLEA 134A, a new refridgerant for A/Cs and refrigerators which is less harmful to the ozone layer.*

- Polar Pumps Ltd, The Brunel Industrial Estate, Blyth Road, Harworth, Doncaster DN11 8QA. 0302 751253. *Manufacture safe-handling, recycling and containment equipment for CFCs.*

- Dean and Wood Ltd, Mole Business Park, Station Road, Leatherhead, Surrey KT22 7BA. 0372 378788. *Market 'thermal' recovery units.*

- Refridgerant Reclaim Ltd, Unit 17, Sandalheath Industrial Estate, Fordingbridge, Hants SP6 1PA. 0425 655818. *Manufacture portable units, to reclaim both CFCs and halon—you can also hire machines.*

37 No Panes No Gains

Over 40% of the energy needed to cool a typical office is due to heat gain through the windows.

Your office window isn't just a sheet of glass—it's an energy system.

It controls the flow of hot or cold air that comes into your office from outdoors.

If it traps heat inside during the winter, you'll be able to run the heating system less. But if it traps heat inside during the summer, you'll have to use more air-conditioning.

A few relatively simple, inexpensive improvements to office windows can make a big difference in how much energy you use, how comfortable employees are, and how much your company spends on heating and cooling.

Glass Acts

■ Sunlight coming through windows produces welcome heat. But in summer, that heat is unwanted. The air-conditioning used to remove it each year could account for 30–40% of your energy bill. One solution: covering windows with shades.

■ Windows need to be shaded in winter, too. Heat loss through windows at night can be reduced by as much as 70% by 'managing' your glass.

Simple Things to Do

■ The easiest and cheapest solution: install reflective film over as many windows as possible. This can cut winter heat loss by 30% and screens out as much as 75% of the sun's rays—which cuts air-conditioning needs.

■ Shades or blinds also reduce heating and cooling costs considerably.

- If you're building or refurbishing invest in double-glazed, low emissivity paned windows. They can pay for themselves immediately; computer simulation programmes can tell you whether you can buy smaller (and less expensive) heating and air-conditioning systems as a result.

Success Stories

✔ The Spitfire and Hurricane Memorial building at RAF Manston experienced problems with an uncomfortably warm summer temperature due to large high level windows. Exhibits were also fading because of UV damage. The installation of solar control film has solved both problems. Heat gain has been reduced by 72%, glare by 78% and UV damage by 74%. A recent cafeteria extension has been similarly treated with the additional benefit of providing insulation—reducing winter heat loss by 34%.

✔ When Greenpeace refurbished their London headquarters they used low emissivity double-glazed glass for the 1400 panes in the building. The naturally ventilated office will save about £400 per year on energy bills because of reduced heat loss.

The Bottom Line

For Your Company

*Windows are a key part of any building's energy system. Whilst an investment in windows or shades can be substantial many improvements yield a quick return on investment.

For the Earth

*According to Pilkingtons, if all single-glazed windows in homes in the UK were changed to double-glazing with low emissivity Pilkington K Glass, energy worth £1 billion would be saved each year.

This energy is equal to the output of three large modern power stations and would reduce CO_2 emissions by 10 million tons a year.

Resources

■ Pilkington Glass Ltd, Prescot Road, St Helens WA10 3TT. 0744 692000. *Make 'Pilkington K' glass.*

■ 3M, 3M House, P.O. Box 1, Market Place, Bracknell, Berks RG12 1JU. 0344 858426. *Manufacturers of 'Solar Control Film'.*

38 Recycle the Rest

About half of the waste an average company produces can be recycled.

If you've already got a paper recycling system in place, you're probably ready to move on to other things.

It's easy to find more rubbish you can rescue from the skip—glass, plastic, aluminium, telephone directories, corrugated cardboard. There may even be recyclables that are unique to your business.

The Second Time Around

■ Recycling your newspaper every day for a year can keep an estimated 13 pounds of air pollution out of the atmosphere.

■ Recycled telephone directories can be made into animal bedding and insulation.

■ A recycled aluminium can is generally reprocessed and back on the shelf in less than six weeks.

■ Glass never wears out, it can be recycled forever.

Simple Things to Do

■ Make a list of the things your company uses that can be recycled.

■ Check with your purchasing department. They can provide you with a list of the manufacturing or office supplies they buy each month. How many are being thrown out that could be recycled?

■ Contact a waste exchange (see One Man's Waste. . . —page 150) or a local recycler to find out which of the items can be recycled.

■ Find out how to prepare materials for recycling. For example, you may need to separate glass by colour, crush metal cans or bag or tie newspapers.

■ Recycle other material the way you recycle office paper. Select a recycler, collect the material and store it in a central location until it can be picked up.

■ If you are only one of several tenants in a building, approach the management about getting everyone interested in recycling.

Success Stories

✔ 3M estimate a saving of £46,760 in 1991 on the cost of land-fill from reclaiming and recycling waste. At their largest manufacturing site at Gorseinon buyers have been found for nearly every by-product from the plant's operations—from computer paper to bulk resin bags.

✔ Matsushita Electric UK recycle 14 tons of polystyrene packing they receive with TV tubes every quarter. Previously the waste, which had been refused at landfills and couldn't be burnt because of toxic content, was costing £200 a day to be removed by an end-user.

   The introduction of a new compaction system now means the polystyrene can be broken down, reground and re-used for other products. The company, having solved an environmental problem, have the bonus of saving £60,000 a year on disposal costs.

✔ In 1992 an estimated 2.9 million rental telephones were collected through BT's recycling scheme. The contract, operated by Mayer-Cohen Industries Ltd, recovers 85% by weight of each telephone, producing ABS, acrylic and PVC plastics and a variety of precious metals. The process is saving thousands of tons of recyclable plastics and metals from ending up as landfill.

The Bottom Line

For Your Company

➥ According to some estimates it can cost £50 to pick up, transport and dump a ton of normal waste—and prices are going up. So recycling can save companies tens of thousands of pounds each year.

➥ Some recycled materials are valuable. For example: computer paper can be worth up to £90 a ton, and precious metals like nickel as much as £2,000 a ton.

For the Earth

➥ The benefits of recycling are enormous. Two examples: glass produced from recycled instead of raw material reduces related air pollution by 20% and water pollution by 50%; recycling corrugated cardboard saves about 25% of the energy used to produce it from raw materials.

Resources

■ Check the Yellow Pages (under 'Recycling').

■ 'The National Directory of Recycling Information'; available from: Waste Watch, 68 Grafton Way, London W1P 5LE. 071 383 3320. £9.95 (Oct. 1993 price).

■ 'Don't throw it all away'; available from Friends of the Earth Ltd, 26–28 Underwood Street, London N1 7JQ. 071 490 1555. *A simple guide to waste reduction and recycling. £2.95 (Oct. 1993 price).*

39 A Pallatable Choice

It takes a tree 10 years to grow enough lumber to manufacture one wooden pallet.

Unless you work in a despatch department, you probably never think about pallets. But every year, millions of them are dumped into landfills. Your company can't afford this needless waste—and neither can the Earth.

Get a Load of This

- Each year, British businesses buy about 60 million wooden pallets. Stacked on top of each other, they'd form a pile 3,810 miles into the sky—the equivalent of 16,000 Empire State Buildings.

- Approximately 22 million new wooden pallets are produced a year in the UK, from almost $1^1/2$ million trees.

- Since the estimated cost to transport and dump one ton of waste is £50, British companies could be spending up to £25 million a year just to throw wooden pallets into landfills.

Simple Things to Do

- Cannibalise broken pallets for re-use, either as components to repair salvageable pallets, or as fencing or even as wood chips for mulch or fuel.

- Invest in a machine that can dismantle wrongly sized or broken pallets effectively, minimising waste.

- Ask your contractor to provide a collection service for broken pallets and to re-use the good components.

- Buy pallets made of recycled plastic. They cost 5 to 10 times more than wooden pallets, but can last at least 10 times longer. You can also replace damaged components yourself because many are screwed rather than nailed together. When they're no longer usable, they can be recycled again either as an element in another pallet or into other useful items.

Success Stories

✔ As a solution to their waste problem Pick Pallets in Nottingham developed 'The Green Machine' to dismantle pallets that were broken or in unwanted sizes, thus enabling the timber to be recycled. They now use two machines themselves and have applied for a patent. Payback on the capital expenditure was achieved in six months through waste reduction and self-sufficiency in board for repairs.

✔ British Airways were paying about £1,000 a week to landfill damaged pallets but at the beginning of 1992 arranged with their supplier for broken pallets to be collected and repaired. The majority of components within damaged pallets are now recycled.

The Bottom Line

For Your Company

✎ A 'Green Machine' will involve a capital outlay but will make dismantling wooden pallets and recycling the good wood economical as well as cutting waste disposal bills.

✎ Plastic pallets cost between £27 and £90 and are designed to last for years. If each lasts as long as 10 wooden pallets—as they should—they'll more than pay for themselves.

For the Earth

✎ Recycling wooden pallets or using recyclable plastic pallets can save trees and significantly reduce dumping.

Resources

- 'The Green Machine', available from Gordon J. Pick, Oatfield Lane, Radcliffe-on-Trent, Notts NG12 2AW. 0602 336120.

- Environmental Polymer Products, Bold Industrial Park, Neills Road, Bold, St Helens, Merseyside WA9 4TH. 0744 810001. *Manufacture a range of recycled-plastic pallets.*

Save-a-Cup collect 2,750,000 plastic cups for recycling every week

Only 10% of building materials come from secondary or recycled sources

Over 15 years, IBM has reduced its energy bill for lighting by £3 million through energy-efficient measures

Tipp-Ex have introduced a 'natural' correction fluid which replaces 1,1,1 trichloroethane with a natural solvent

There are over 2,000 clothing banks at sites all over Britain, saving 50,000 tons of material for recycling

In 1992, 1.5 billion steel and 694 million aluminium cans were recycled

40 Green Audit

By 1992, a waste audit undertaken by the Huntsman Chemical Company Ltd had reduced liquid and solid waste by 70% through improved maintenance and operating methods. Disposal costs were reduced by £80,000 and water and other material waste by £100,000 giving a payback on capital investment in around 13 months.

How can you get a clear picture of what your company needs to do to be more environmentally responsible?

Conduct a Green Audit.

Everyone knows what an audit is, but how does it apply to the environment?

A good audit will show you how to conserve water, save materials, and become more energy-efficient. That's good for your business—and the planet.

In the Audit-torium

■ Green Audits didn't even exist a few years ago. They were first created to help industrial companies determine whether they complied with UK and EC environmental laws and directives.

Now they're used by all types of companies.

■ It should be easy for any business to find an 'environmental auditor'. There are more than 340 consultancies and hundreds more individual auditors in the UK.

■ There are different kinds of audits, it depends on what your company needs. The most common audits cover waste, energy and water, but you could also do a transport audit, a hazardous waste audit, a sites and buildings audit or even a product audit.

Who's Going to Do It?

If You Do It Yourself

■ It's less expensive and it's more efficient, because no one knows your company better than the people who work there. However, you may not have the time and expertise to gather all the necessary information.

■ If you've set up a Green Team, it can play a key role by co-ordinating information from every department.

■ Try to be as thorough as possible when gathering information. You cannot make intelligent decisions without detailed data.

■ Keep accurate records of your audit, you may need the information later to show to others. Be sure to date them; that way, you can make comparison audits in a year or two.

■ A camera might come in handy to record your findings.

Go with a Pro

■ It may be more expensive to hire an auditor, but professionals are probably quicker and may think of things you could miss.

■ Plus, experts have the experience to make recommendations on what to do next.

■ Your Green Team can still play a role, acting as a liaison between the expert and the company.

■ Approach the Association of Environmental Consultants or The Institute for Environmental Assessment. They can suggest consultants in your area who meet their codes of practice.

■ In all areas, the local authority and other relevant environmental control authorities will be able to advise—as will your company's Trade Association.

- You should still exercise overall control by defining goals, baselines, scope and priorities of the audit before any consultancy work is undertaken.

A Do-It-Yourself Audit

- There are three parts to a Green Audit: planning, gathering information and recommendations.

- First, decide what you want to know. For example: How much does your company throw away—and how much of it could be recycled? Or, how much energy does your company use, and how could it be used more efficiently?

- Next, create a plan to gather the information. Details will depend on the size of your business. If it's big enough, you could form teams to do the work; if small enough, you can do the work yourself.

- You might need an expert to review your plan.

What to Do Next

- When you've completed your audit, put all the information together into a single report, along with any recommendations.

- Circulate a rough draft among members of the Green Team and ask for their feedback.

- When you've compiled a final report, send a copy to the head of the company or the manager of your facility.

- Make copies available to employees.

Success Story

✔ In December 1992, NatWest completed a project to change the lighting configuration at their King Cross House offices. 10–15-year-old twin fluorescents with prismatic diffusers were replaced with single tubes, high frequency ballasts and reflectors. Louvres were added to meet EC regulations on computer screen glare. Already, it's apparent that savings are likely to be considerable: an estimated £70,000 on electricity, £20,000 on reduced air-conditioning requirements and £20,000 on reduced maintenance. Payback for the eight-week project is expected to be no more than two years. The initiative, in response to a group directive to reduce energy consumption by 15%, was identified as viable by an energy site survey—or energy audit.

The Bottom Line

For Your Company

✐ Conducting a green audit requires an investment—even if it is only management or employee time.

For a consultant, an example for a 400-person, 50,000-square foot manufacturing facility would be £5–10,000. The audit would take 2–4 days on site with a final report usually available in about three weeks. In most cases, the results reveal many ways your company can save money for years to come through more efficient use of resources.

For the Earth

✐ The potential benefits from Green Audits are incalculable, and there's no doubt that they're good for the planet.

Resources

- 'The Directory of Environmental Consultants' 1992/93. Published by Environmental Data Services (ENDS), Finsbury Business Centre, Bowling Green Lane, London EC1R 0NE. 071 278 4745. £33 to subscribers, £49.50 to non-subscribers (Oct. 1993 prices).

- The Institute for Environmental Assessment, Gregory Croft House, Fen Road, East Kirkby, Lincs PE23 4DB. 0790 3613. *They can put you in touch with an auditor qualified for your requirements.*

- The Association of Environmental Consultants, P.O. Box 472, St Albans, Herts AL1 1AD. 0727 853498.

Through the recycling of waste water at their latex plant in Kings Lynn, Dow Chemicals have reduced the amount of sludge sent to landfill by 90%

The SC Johnson corporation removed CFCs from its aerosols in 1975— long before the threats to the ozone layer were common knowledge

Tesco Stores Ltd have introduced a new car wash system which recycles water, reducing fresh water required for each wash from 46 gallons to just two

Annual water bills at ICI's Ardeer site in Scotland have been cut by £6,000 following suggestions by employees

Exel Logistics have 'Environmental Champions' at all their sites within the UK

41 Make It a Matter of Policy

A 1990 survey found that only 20% of Britons believe that British industry is sufficiently concerned about the environment.

Your company has all kinds of policies—pay-roll and personnel, salary and sick leave. There are policies about jury duty, overtime, maternity leave and a dozen other things.

Now it's time to establish a policy to protect the environment.

Hidden Agenda?

■ First, find out whether your company has any written policies about the environment.

■ If they have, let others know. Ask to have the policy posted or reprinted in the company newsletter.

Assurance Policy

■ If none exists, ask management to consider adopting a policy. If they know employees are interested, they might be receptive.

■ Offer to help draft a policy.

■ Let anyone who's interested have a hand in writing it. Ask for suggestions. What are the important issues? What can different departments do to establish realistic guidelines?

■ Organise informal discussions during which people can share ideas and debate some of the issues.

■ Build in flexibility; the policy doesn't have to be permanent. It can be amended as new technologies and laws emerge.

Pass It Around

■ Give everyone a chance to read the first draft and to offer comments.

- Print or summarise the completed policy statement in your company publications, catalogues and annual report. Make sure it appears in the employees' handbook and that it is given to all employees.

Success Stories

✔ British Telecom's Environmental Policy Statement commits the organisation to producing an annual environmental performance report, which aims to be a self-critical and open review of BT's operations and how they affect the environment.

Each year, targets are set and then quantified against their success rates. In 1992, 36 targets were set with 26 successfully met before schedule.

The targets in the 1993 report include: support for research and development into adhesives suitable for making telephone directories generally recyclable; to have an aluminium can collection point at every main BT building and to provide 80% of BT managers with video conferencing studios by May 1993.

✔ The S.C. Johnson Corporation has included the environment in its business philosophy statements since 1976. Current company objectives to be achieved by 1995, using 1990 figures as a base, include reducing air emissions, water effluents and solid waste disposal from manufacturing operations by 50% and recycling nearly all paper, cardboard, glass and steel materials used in manufacturing and office facilities in the UK.

The Bottom Line

For Your Company

✎ Polls show that your customers are looking for companies to do more to help the environment. They say that customers will change their buying habits to favour firms that are environmentally sensitive. Your policy represents your promise, to employees, customers and the communities where you do business, that you will do all you can to protect the Earth.

✍ It is obvious, but we have to say it in this book at least once. No Earth, no customers.

For the Earth

✍ Your commitment will help encourage others to take protecting the planet more seriously.

✍ However, it's not just your commitment, but the way you follow through that counts. The products you sell, the services you provide and the way you conduct business all have an immediate impact on the Earth.

British Gas have produced 14 booklets on environmental issues for the public

The Ethical Investors Group pledge 50% of their profits to charities nominated by their clients

The Bodyshop is cutting the use of company cars as perks. For essential use only two models are available; the Volkswagen Golf 'Umwelt' and the Audi Turbo diesel generally reckoned to be the least polluting cars available

Universal Office Supplies now have over 200 green products available

The Centre for Exploitation of Science and Technology (CEST) estimate the market for environmental technology and services to be £140 billion between 1991 and 2000

---

42 Stay at Home (Teleworking)

It has been estimated that by the mid 1990s over 2 million people could be working remotely, either from home or from small satellite offices.

It's six o'clock and time to go home. The day, as usual, is already 12 hours old because of the hour-long journey this morning to make that 8.15 a.m. conference call with Japan. In fact the day has been a succession of calls and meetings—you've spent several hours on the telephone.

Just stop to think—couldn't you have done all of this at home?

'On the Dis-Assembly Line'

- BT's teleworking research group estimates that the average commuter would save 16% of his or her annual energy bill by teleworking at home—that's the equivalent of 135 gallons of petrol or 1.53 tons of CO_2 not released into the atmosphere.

- Companies are paying up to £8,000 per person, per year in building costs (space heating and lighting and floor space rent). Working from home would reduce this cost to zero.

- The electronics revolution has made it relatively simple to link remote areas to information systems via the telephone line. Home terminals can now be serviced by an Integrated Service Digital Network (ISDN) which can transmit and receive high speed, high quality voice, data, image and text down a single copper wire.

Simple Things to Do

- Quantify the actual and potential overheads associated with employing staff in offices which would be eliminated by teleworking—you could also make allowances for increased productivity (estimates range from 10–60%), lower absenteeism and the retention of valuable skills (e.g. married women with children, disabled people and disaffected commuters).

- Once you've been converted by the benefits, research the Information Technology (IT) requirements necessary to get the scheme off the ground.

- Run a pilot scheme—ask for volunteers. You may be inundated—according to recent research 67% of 25–34 year olds are positive about teleworking .

- Make sure the pilot scheme is well managed. One of the main problems associated with teleworking is the isolation felt by some practitioners who have lost the social benefits of the office environment. Managerial input should be weekly. In an experiment run by BT, 10 directory enquiry operators working from home were linked together by videophones to counter any feelings of isolation. Nine of the 10 wanted to continue when the experiment was concluded.

Success Stories

✔ ICL began offering teleworking to its staff in 1969 as a pragmatic solution to an internal problem—the loss of women bringing up children—a valuable resource the company wanted to keep.

There are now about 350 trained analysts working remotely for ICL, the majority within a subsidiary, Contract Programming Services (CPS). Although a large proportion are still women, a growing number of male staff are now adopting teleworking for reasons ranging from doing courses to running hill-farms in Wales.

✔ Many of IBM's UK employees are affected by SMART, the company's forward looking policy of decentralising its staff operations and cutting its second-highest cost—office space.

As a prime mover in the electronics business IBM saw the advantages in providing some staff with work stations either at home or in satellite offices where they can access their mail and files.

As a result the company expects to be allocating one desk to three or four staff and believes it can cut building costs by over 25% as well as reducing fuel and paper consumption.

✔ The London Borough of Enfield introduced home working in 1989 to cope with the introduction of the Poll Tax. There are now 58 clerical teleworkers linked to the central main frame. The Borough has calculated a saving of £50,000 but sees this as less important than the benefits of having a committed, stable workforce.

The Bottom Line

For Your Company

✍ Teleworking is the future. Advances in computer and communications technology have made it possible to reduce building and transport costs for employees whilst offering them greater flexibility.

One financial company, who operated a 20-person teleworking pilot scheme, estimated annual savings of £20,000 per employee.

✍ Working in crowded, closed environments is not good for health—Sick Building Syndrome is now officially recognised as a problem.

Neither is the stress caused by commuting. Teleworkers are reported to lose less than the average number of days to sickness—through greater freedom of choice comes greater commitment.

For the Earth

✍ If just 1% of the working population adopted teleworking we could save almost 300,000 tons of CO_2 from being emitted just through the reduction in the number of cars used for commuting.

Resources

■ 'The Telecommuters' by Francis Kinsman; 'Teleworking Explained' by Gray, Hodson and Gordon. Both books are published by and are available from John Wiley & Sons Ltd, Baffins Lane, Chichester, West Sussex PO19 1UD. 0243 779777. Price £24.95 and £29.95 (Oct. 1993 prices).

■ Henley Management College, Greenlands, Henley-on-Thames, Oxfordshire RG9 3AU. 0491 571454. *A business school with an interest in future ways of work. Telephone for membership details of 'The Future Work Forum'.*

43 Let the Sun Shine In

Office buildings consume 20% of all electricity used in the UK.

People have been talking about the enormous potential of solar power for years. Many of the early predictions haven't been fulfilled yet, but in some areas, solar energy is already a reliable source of power. It's no longer science fiction—it's here.

Rays of Hope

- According to the Solar Trade Association about 45,000 buildings in the UK use solar hot water heaters. Although applications have so far been mainly domestic, business usage is growing fast.

- Some building techniques help to capture the sun's rays as a source of heat. These techniques are called 'passive' solar because they don't require special equipment; using them can cut heating costs by up to 50%.

- Sunlight can be harnessed to operate lights, signs and a variety of electrical appliances. This process of converting sunlight directly to electricity is called 'photovoltaics'.

- Solar calculators use photovoltaics. More than a million of them were sold in the UK in 1992.

Simple Things to Do

- Set up a solar water heating system. A 120-gallon tank will cost about £5,000. Savings could be as much as 60% of your water heating bill.

- Learn about other applications where photovoltaics can provide electricity. As costs come down and conventional power prices go up more applications will become viable.

■ Building a new facility? Ask your architect to incorporate 'passive' solar designs that make maximum use of sun and shade. Manage windows to maximise light and minimise heating and cooling costs.

Success Story

✔ Strathclyde University utilised a transparent insulation material that converts daylight into useful heat in a new student residence building. The passive solar design performs like a giant storage heater resulting in heating costs about half of what would normally be expected—a saving equivalent to £40,000 a year.

The Bottom Line

For Your Company

🖋 While solar technology is still improving, there are opportunities to save money and energy with it now. You can start using solar energy at any level, from a £7 solar battery charger or calculator to security lighting for around £100 or a more expensive water heating system.

For the Earth

🖋 Every kilowatt of power generated by solar energy means burning that much less oil, coal or natural gas.

Resources

- Solar Trade Association, 'Pengillan', Lerryn, Lostwithiel, Cornwall PL22 0QE. 0208 873518.

- Thermomax Solar Energy Systems, 'Rayotec', London Road, Sunningdale, Ascot SL5 0DJ. 0344 874747. *Manufacture, supply and install solar hot water systems.*

- Energy Technology Support Unit (ETSU), Harwell Laboratory, Oxon OX11 0RA. 0235 432450. *An excellent source of information and advice on passive solar techniques and the 'Thermie' programme, which can provide financial support for passive solar projects.*

Amblers of Ballyclare eliminated the use of 35,000 plastic bags a week (used to protect yarn) with no loss of product quality—and saved £15,000 a year

Jaegar Tailoring are raising employee awareness by including environmental messages in payslips

Simpson, Wright & Lowe used employee teams to examine their production cycle in 1991/92; wasted raw materials were reduced by 30%, saving £100,000

NatWest's 1991/92 trial of producing 40,000 current account statements from 60% recycled paper is continuing

44 Wilderness Incorporated

95% of the UK's wildflower meadows were lost before the mid 1980s. The remaining fraction is being lost at a rate of 10% a year according to the RSNC Wildlife Trusts Partnership.

We're not sure where the term 'greenspace' came from, but it's one that business ought to know.

It refers to land—developed or not—that's used to support plants and wildlife. This can mean anything from planting a few trees near a warehouse to preserving a wetland.

Since British companies control so much property, they can have a huge impact by establishing greenspace wherever possible.

Trees Please

■ Trees and other plants play a major role in cleaning the air and slowing down global warming. For example: a mature tree absorbs an average of 13 pounds of carbon dioxide each year.

■ Trees are an effective way of shielding buildings from noise and solar gain. The shade given by trees in summer will reduce your air-conditioning use as well as being aesthetically pleasing.

■ Since 1800, 19 plant species have become extinct in the UK because of human activity. Another 51 are currently classed as 'vulnerable'.

Simple Things to Do

■ Create as much greenspace as possible around your company's facilities. Look at car parks, fields, abandoned facilities and other places that can be planted and developed.

■ Launch a company-wide (or facility-wide) campaign to turn an abandoned area into a park. Employees can raise funds and even do planting and construction themselves.

- If your company has unused or underused land, consider turning it into a wildlife refuge, perhaps incorporating a pond or lake for wildfowl and aquatic life. If appropriate, open the land to the public.

- If your company is developing land, try to compensate by preserving an equal, or greater, sized plot for wildlife.

Success Stories

✔ The BP Kent Environmental Reserve was initiated in 1990 at the Isle of Grain Distribution Terminal now operated by Air BP. The project has utilised an area of unused land to establish natural habitats for plants, mammals, birds, butterflies and even reptiles. A freshwater lagoon was extended and new ponds excavated, one specifically as a nesting area for ringed plovers. Over 200 trees and shrubs were planted including ash, alder, rowan, holly and hazel.

The site is maintained by the Wildlife Consultants IEM, employee volunteers and by local enthusiasts. It is now a resource not only for the company and its employees but also for the local community.

✔ Crewe Business Park, awarded 'Wildlife Pond of the Year 1992' by the Wildfowl and Wetlands Trust, amazingly uses only 25% of its total area for business development. The remainder includes wildflower meadows and natural habitats for owls, foxes, badgers, kingfishers, mallards and some species of dragonfly.

The Bottom Line

For Your Company

✍ It is far cheaper to maintain a native landscape than traditional turf grass, exotics and seasonal flower beds.

If your land is unused it will cost you very little to manage it and it will give immeasurable bonuses—better staff morale and a better public perception of your company—and, after all, the wildlife comes free!

For the Earth

_About 300 native plants are in danger of becoming extinct in Britain. Greenspace can give them a home.

Resources

■ Industrial Environment Management (IEM), Suite 1, The Mill, 1 Old Road, Linslade, Leighton Buzzard, Beds LU7 7RB. 0525 372562. *A consultancy who will help you to introduce and manage nature areas on industrial sites.*

■ 'Countryside Stewardship', The Countryside Commission, John Dower House, Crescent Place, Cheltenham, Gloucestershire GL50 3RA. 0242 521381. *Discretionary grants are available to manage land for conservation.*

■ The Groundwork Foundation, 85–87 Cornwall Street, Birmingham B3 3BY. 021 2368565.

■ RSNC, The Wildlife Trusts Partnership, The Green, Witham Park, Waterside South, Lincoln LN5 7JR. 0522 544400.

45 The Three Rs (Training)

A survey undertaken by David Bellamy Associates in 1992 indicated that only 20% of respondents had received any staff training on green issues.

You have an environmental policy approved by the board, but how are you going to get staff awareness and support to put meat on the bones? Training should start with the chief executive and filter through to all levels of management and employees.

Who Needs It?

- Chief executives need to know that good environmental performance is good business sense.

- Company secretaries need to know the legal requirements and whether or not these requirements are being met.

- Production directors need to know if their facilities are operating as efficiently as possible.

- General staff need to know about changes in work practices and the ideas behind the company's policy. In many cases it is they who can quickly spot waste and inefficiency and recommend improvements.

Simple Things to Do

- Assess the level of existing knowledge on the environment before deciding on a training strategy—it is possible you could utilise existing knowledge and expertise.

- If there isn't an appropriate level of understanding, approach external specialists. Some of the options available: environmental consultants, business seminars and breakfast clubs, lectures and courses run by universities, business organisations and environmental training groups.

■ Consider sending delegates on specific modules that would be of benefit to your company.

Success Stories

✔ Driven by a policy laid down by the main board, P&O have developed a comprehensive training provision on environmental issues which can be split into four levels.

First, the priority was to acquaint directors and senior management from each of the P&O companies with basic environmental issues. This was achieved through an initial two-day course with a further follow-up course planned.

Secondly, personnel responsible for carrying out environmental assessments were selected for a series of courses run by environmental consultants.

Thirdly, one-day environmental awareness courses are run internally on a regular basis for supervisors and managers.

Finally, an environmental module is now an integrated part of the general management development programme.

As Dr Mike Monaghan, Director for Environment stated, 'Environmental Training is not "Stand-Alone" at P&O, it's part of our general management programme.'

✔ Millican Contract Carpets, who make carpet tiles for commercial use, see staff awareness as an essential component in spotting inefficiencies in their production process.

People work in teams, and waste minimisation awareness is stimulated at meetings by each team's facilitator.

Good communication and the involvement of all staff have been major factors in reducing solid waste tonnage by over 50% since 1990.

The Bottom Line

For Your Company

➤ Graduates, your main source of management trainees, are concerned about the environmental performance of prospective employers. Of 50,000 new graduates in 1991, 56% felt that a company's environmental policy was important when choosing their careers.

➤ The shopfloor employee who develops an energy efficiency idea will save your company money.

For the Earth

➤ Every time a member of your workforce considers the environmental impact of an action or process, he or she is making a valuable contribution toward conserving the Earth's resources.

Resources

■ The Environment Council, 21 Elizabeth Street, London SW1W 9RP. 071 824 8411. *Produce a list of environmental courses.*

■ CAPITB plc, Business Development Dept, 80 Richards Lane, Pudsey, Leeds LS28 6BN. 0532 393355. *Provide training modules for small, medium or large companies, to be run externally or in-house.*

■ The Field Studies Council, Preston Montford, Montford Bridge, Shrewsbury SY4 1DX. 0743 850380. *An environmental training organisation.*

■ Losehill Hall, Peak National Study Centre, Castleton, Derbys S30 2WB. 0433 620373. *Provide a full portfolio on environmental courses for industry.*

■ 'Environmental Education and Training' — a booklet giving guidelines to business available from the CBI, Centre Point, 103 New Oxford Street, London. WC1A 1DU. 071 379 7400. Price £2.50 for members, £5 for non-members (Oct. 1993 prices).

NatWest Markets HQ at Bishopsgate produces 50 large stacks of paper waste for recycling every day

Coutts and Co. have phased out halon fire extinguishers

15 of Uden Associates' 27 staff cycle to the firm's offices at Chelsea Wharf every day

The Woodland Trust have received over £200,000 through its affinity card with Royal Bank of Scotland

NatWest are holding discussions with local transport companies about re-routing buses into newly formed business parks

46 Don't Waste Away

Each year, British industry generates roughly 100 pounds of hazardous waste for every UK citizen.

Is your business creating hazardous waste? It might be and you might not even know it—it is a legal requirement to know.

Unfortunately, you can't expect to eliminate all hazardous substances overnight—they're used in the production of almost everything, e.g. computers, videotapes and medications. With the help of new methods and technologies, companies are beginning to cut down on the amount of toxins they generate—and much more waste reduction is possible.

Cleaning Up Your Act

- According to British 'special waste' regulations, even businesses that produce small quantities of hazardous waste must send out notification to their waste regulation authority for clearance.

- There is no totally 'safe' way to dispose of these wastes. Even the best landfills might eventually leak.

- In 1992 the landfill of 'special waste' cost British industry about £40 million. The costs of dealing with hazardous material will continue to grow as more disposal sites close, pollution control regulations get tougher and liabilities increase.

- The best solution: waste minimisation. Hundreds of British companies are discovering that they can reduce raw material, production and disposal costs, whilst increasing their efficiency and profits.

Simple Things to Do

Identify the Problem

- Conduct a waste audit: find out where toxins are being used or produced in your company; identify alternatives that can reduce total toxin output.

- Need Help? Contact the DTI's Environment Unit, Green Business Clubs or Environmental Consultancies.

Minimise Toxins

- Redesign your products, if feasible, so they require fewer toxic materials. For example, instead of designing a product that must be painted, use a base material that doesn't need painting.

- Redesign the process: use less hazardous materials. For example, substitute a water-based ink for a metal-based one; clean metal surfaces with a mechanical abrasive instead of a chemical solvent.

- Involve all employees. Increasing workforce awareness and commitment can be instrumental in making a success of a waste reduction initiative.

Recycle or Re-use Hazardous Materials

- You may be able to re-use some of your hazardous materials on site. Some companies extract and re-use precious metals, solvents and lubricants.

- Contact a waste-broker to find out if you can sell or trade waste by-products to other companies.

Dispose of Wastes Properly

- Separate hazardous waste early, before it gets mixed into other effluent. This makes it easier to target toxic material for appropriate treatment and to dispose of the non-hazardous portion.

- Investigate new technologies for separating or neutralising hazardous wastes. Industrial scientists are experimenting with various techniques to destroy harmful compounds or feed them to chemical-eating microbes.

Success Stories

✔ 3M's 'Pollution Prevention Pays (3P)' programme has resulted in the annual elimination of 5,012 tons of air pollutants, 2,350 tons of sludge and solid waste and savings of over £8.2 million for the company. 3M also sets pollution reduction goals and in 1990 initiated 'Challenge 95' which aims for a 35% reduction in waste generated by 1995.

✔ Eastern Counties Leather plc developed a new degreasing system which eliminated the need for solvents, saving on cost, pollution and the exposure of employees to a toxic chemical. As a result of eliminating solvents, their chamois leather now has a 70% water absorption ability, giving them a distinct edge over their competitors.

The Bottom Line

For Your Company

✐ By taking better charge of toxins, your company can avoid fines, costly litigation, bad public relations and possible lawsuits against company officials.

✍ By reducing the amount of hazardous waste generated, you can make dramatic savings on transporting and disposing of waste, as well as on new pollution control equipment.

✍ Waste reduction means lower exposure of your workforce to toxins. This can reduce sickness and compensation claims.

✍ 'Waste is frequently the by-product of inefficiency in the system. Stopping or reducing waste contributes to improved efficiency. Minimising waste should maximise profits.'— Michael Heseltine.

For the Earth

✍ 70% of drinking water in England and Wales comes from rivers and streams. Improper disposal of hazardous waste can pollute these controlled waters. Reducing hazardous waste will mean a safer water supply.

Resources

■ Department of Trade and Industry (DTI) Environmental Helpline. Freephone 0800 585 794.

■ Waste Facility Audit Association; contact the Environmental Assessment Group Ltd, 31 Dover Street, London W1X 3RA. 071 495 0576. *They can audit your waste streams and match you with companies who have compatible materials to dispose of at a fraction of the cost of an external consultant.*

47 A Green Blueprint

Britain spends about £400 million a year on tropical hardwoods.

Planning a new building? Refurbishing your office? You're probably more concerned abouth the cost than anything else. However, your choice of building materials and the way in which you dispose of construction wastes are important, too.

A growing number of builders and designers are concerned with how their work—siting, design and the waste systems they install—affects the environment.

If you're not involved in the design and construction process in your company, why not pass this along to the people who are?

Did You Know?

- Many types of plywood and particle board emit formaldehyde, a known carcinogen.

- Construction affects the rainforests. Much of the rainforest wood imported into the UK arrives in the form of plywood and panelling, often used in the construction of new buildings.

- Foam insulation used on roofs and pipes may contain ozone-depleting CFCs.

- Loose soil from construction sites is a major contributor to 'run-off' pollution in streams and rivers.

Simple Things to Do

When Planning Sites and Landscaping

- Take maximum advantage of sunlight for lighting and passive solar heating.

- Plant deciduous trees on the south side to provide summer shade; also shade roofs, air-conditioning coils and windows.

When Selecting Materials

- Consult the Association of Environment Conscious Building for advice on choosing materials that do the least harm in their harvesting or mining, use and disposal.

- Try to use reclaimed materials.

- Use materials that do not require toxic protective coating or treatments.

- Avoid petro-chemical based paints and try to find substitutes for vinyl floor and wall coverings, particle boards, and certain types of carpets, which can all emit dangerous chemicals.

- Try to limit purchases of timber to 'certified' woods, from suppliers practising sustainable rainforest management.

During Construction

- Protect trees and other vegetation. Be sure the whole crew is alerted to tree-saving steps like avoiding soil compaction over (and excavation near) roots.

- Reduce soil run-off into streams or waterways by retaining as much ground cover as possible. Erect barriers at the edge of the site to trap runaway soils.

- Consider donating surplus building materials to an organisation that builds housing for low-income or homeless people. Do not throw it away.

Success Story

- ✔ The design and building of Woodhouse Medical Centre in Sheffield was approached in a holistic way by architects Brenda and Robert Vale. The concept, to build a green building within the budget of a conventional one, was achieved through using maximum insulation to reduce fossil fuel demand, utilising passive solar gain, using local materials to minimise transport costs and using materials with a low manufacturing energy demand, long life and minimum maintenance.

The building uses no tropical hardwoods, CFCs or high toxic preservatives, whilst employing low emissivity glass, compact fluorescent bulbs and roof lights to minimise energy consumption—heat loss was 76% lower than building regulations stipulated at the time.

The recipient of 'Green Building of the Year' in 1992 it was built with slight modifications of traditional UK construction methods for an equivalent price to a building with no green features.

The Bottom Line

For Your Company

✒ Buying organic paints, linoleum instead of vinyl floor coverings, formaldehyde-free particle board or non-toxic preservatives may cost your company a little more but will help you get clean air in your building—reducing absenteeism and increasing productivity.

For the Earth

✒ Adopting different design approaches and building materials will 'help to reduce global warming, ozone depletion, energy consumption, air and water pollution and solid waste'—The American Institute of Architects.

✒ Billions of pounds are spent each year on construction and interior design materials. If more businesses change their purchasing habits, suppliers will have a stronger incentive to shift to environmentally sensitive materials.

Resources

■ Association of Environment Conscious Building, Windlake House, Westend, Coaley, Gloucestershire GL11 5DX. 0453 890757. *An excellent information source who also publish 'Greener Building', an updatable looseleaf directory of products and services. Price £31.50 (Oct. 1993).*

■ Ecological Design Association, 20 High Street, Stroud, Gloucestershire GL5 1AS. 0453 765575. *Produce a directory and newsletter and run lectures, seminars, workshops and visits to eco-projects.*

48 One Man's Waste...

Scottish Power plc has set up a new business to sell their main by-product, pulverised fuel ash, as a replacement for cement and aggregates in a wide range of products. So far over 400,000 tons have been recycled.

Got any brewery sludge, used industrial lubricants or plastic nappy trimmings around? Would you believe there are companies that would love to have them?

It's true. Increasingly, manufacturers are finding uses for waste products from other industries.

How do you find a company to work with? 'Waste Exchanges'. If anyone can help you, they can.

Wasting Away

■ British industry produces about 84 million tons of scrap paper, wood, plastic and other non-hazardous waste each year. They also produce 2.5 million tons of 'special' waste. Only a small fraction of this waste is recycled.

■ These discards can be used in surprising ways. For example, plastic waste can be moulded into park benches, shredded paper used as animal bedding, and old tyres turned into carpet underlay or road filling material.

■ British companies are looking long and hard at alternatives to landfill as space gets more expensive and difficult to find. 'Waste exchanges' which match buyers and sellers are beginning to appear. One, 'Waste Exchange Services' based in Cleveland, has been called the 'Date-Line' of the waste world.

Simple Things to Do

■ Quantify what waste you're producing and what it's costing you. If you measure it you manage it.

- Look at separating solids or 'special' waste before disposal—it could be valuable. Some metals can be worth thousands of pounds per ton.

- Try placing an advert in a trade publication. One man's waste is another man's raw material.

- Contact a waste exchange. They publish listings or can put your company onto a database which could either find you a match quickly or identify new processes and markets for your by-product.

Work Out the Details

- Everything is negotiable, from the purchase price to transportation of the waste.

- Take note: if you're selling a hazardous waste it's up to the companies involved to look into the legal aspects of the 'duty of care', licences to reprocess and waste transfer documentation.

Success Story

✔ Advance Tapes Ltd, a Leicester company producing adhesive tapes, used to landfill about 3 tons of PVC edge trim a week. An extrusion and re-granulation plant has produced material suitable for re-use in various ways, one of which is in the forming of shoe soles.

Their original aim to break even and not landfill PVC has been surpassed. Reprocessing saves disposal costs of £8,000 per year, whilst the material reclaimed has a value of £40,000!

The Bottom Line

For Your Company

⚖ Waste disposal costs are mounting as landfill sights become exhausted. Non-hazardous material disposal averages £8 a ton whilst hazardous material disposal can cost up to £40 a ton. With prices expected to double in the next few years it is going to become more and more economically viable to recycle waste rather than to dump it.

For the Earth

⚖ Recycling prevents pollution by reducing the amount of waste discarded in landfills, burned in incinerators, treated in sewage plants or dumped illegally. It also makes the most of resources we already have.

Resources

■ Waste Exchange Services, 8 Stockton Enterprise Centre, 7 Brunswick Street, Stockton-on-Tees TS18 1DW. 0642 603726. *Produce a newsletter and run a database. Charges are usually 15% of the first year's savings in disposal costs.*

■ Green Base Exchange, 47 Arrowsmith Road, Chigwell, Essex IG7 4PJ. 081 501 1242. *An on-line industrial waste exchange. Companies can log on and place an unlimited number of adverts for waste and second-hand equipment as well as receiving a comprehensive environmental briefing. Subscriptions are £51.50 a year (Oct. 1993 price).*

49 Cut Water

British industry uses over a billion gallons of fresh water every day. That's enough to fill all the baths in Greater London—morning and night.

Water is crucial to thousands of industries. You cannot walk through a car plant, a textile mill or a food processing company without seeing it flowing through the manufacturing process.

In the past, the easiest thing for a company to do was dump dirty water into local sewers and let treatment plants deal with it, but laws are getting tougher and water is becoming more scarce and more expensive.

Many companies are finding it pays either to recycle their water or to look at other minimisation ideas.

This isn't a project for an average office worker—it can be capital intensive and a highly specialised operation. It is, however, an important one for business to tackle, and that's why we've included it here.

Did You Know?

- We use about 300 billion gallons of water a year in industrial processes.

- That water costs companies nearly £1 billion a year.

- It takes 24 gallons of water to make one pound of plastic, 55 gallons to make one pound of synthetic rubber, 150 gallons to process one barrel of beer, 5,400 gallons to make one car tyre and 35,500 gallons to produce one car.

- Some industrial waste water contains toxic chemicals like benzene or chlorine which aren't completely filtered out at waste water plants. The result: these chemicals can get into rivers or even back into our drinking water—but this water could be re-used for manufacturing purposes.

Simple Things to Do

- Do a waste water audit. Ask how much water is being discharged and what it contains.

- Find a consultant. Since every system is unique, you need someone who is knowledgeable about your industrial process.

- Check with your company's trade association; someone might have already done your research for you.

THIS MACHINE TURNS WASTE LIQUID INTO DRINKING WATER...
... AND VICE VERSA!

Success Stories

✔ In 1990, ICI Paints in Stowmarket were sending 3 million litres of wash-water to landfill because of its small content of caustic soda. The introduction of a new process to segregate the caustic soda led to a 50% cost saving by 1992. Meanwhile, ICI Watercare were developing a new ultra-filtration membrane system.

Now introduced, this system has virtually completely separated solids from waste water, creating double-edged benefits. Clean water is available to recycle for further washings and the by-product of the process is a marketable commodity. The volume of waste water is now negligible, saving £100,000 a year, with a similar figure generated from the sale of the by-product.

✔ At one of Courtaulds Textiles' dyehouses, the volume of water used in processing has been halved whilst maintaining production of the same meterage of fabric.

The reductions have been achieved by attention to issues including liquor ratios, measurement of flows, critical calibration of pumps and metres, reviews of process routes and effluent management.

✔ The Aire and Calder project is a waste water minimisation club. Most of the companies—drawn from the chemicals, manufacturing, soft drinks, printing, engineering and commercial laundry industries—have, in their first year, identified savings worth tens of thousands of pounds annually. Many of the options are extremely simple and can be implemented quickly. 'Tens of thousands' according to one participant, 'simply by the turn of a valve'.

The Bottom Line

For Your Company

✎ Recycling and minimising water can cut water use by 25–70%. In addition, it reduces the possibility of discharging contaminated waste.

For the Earth

✎ Less than 1% of the Earth's surface is made up of liquid freshwater. We may not be in danger of running out of water, but we are short on water that's clean enough to drink and close enough to use.

Resources

■ Centre for the Exploitation of Science and Technology (CEST), 5 Berners Road, London N1 0PW. 071 354 9944. *Initiated the Aire and Calder project and will be running workshops and conferences on the findings.*

■ British Effluent and Water Association (BEAWA), 5 Castle Street, High Wycombe, Bucks HP13 6RZ. 0494 444544. *Its members are manufacturers of water (and/or waste water) equipment.*

50 Spread the Word

If you've made it through this book, you've already invested time and energy in changing the way you do business.

Here's something else you can do: spread the word; let other business people know there are things they can do right now to help protect the environment.

There is no question that the 1990s are a critical point in human history. We can make a commitment to keep the Earth safe and inhabitable for future generations—or let it continue to deteriorate.

Businesses have more power to do either of these than any other institution in our society.

DO WE REALLY HAVE A CHOICE?

To help you make the necessary changes the Department of Trade and Industry has an environmental helpline for businesses. Telephone calls are free. 0800 585794.

Greenleaf Publishing Recommends

■ 'CONSERVERS AT WORK'—A membership scheme for individuals in the workplace run by the Environment Council. The cost is £17 (Oct. 1993 price) to join, for which you receive a book, newsletter, helpline and details of seminars. 'Conservers' learn how to save energy, water and materials used in their daily work. Contact The Environment Council, 21 Elizabeth Street, London SW1W 9RP. 071 824 8411.

■ WARMER BULLETIN—Acts as a world-wide information service to encourage the recycling of materials and energy from post-consumer waste. It is published quarterly and is available free of charge from 'The Warmer Campaign', 83 Mount Ephraim, Tunbridge Wells, Kent TN4 8BS. 0892 524626.

■ ENVIRONMENTAL DATA SERVICES REPORT (ENDS)—This monthly bulletin covers environmental issues across the spectrum—legislation, waste management, recycling, energy and news in comprehensive fashion. Subscription rates are currently £128 for new subscribers, thereafter £197. Contact Environmental Data Services Ltd, Unit 24, Finsbury Business Centre, 40 Bowling Green Lane, London EC1R 0NE. 071 278 4745.

■ CBI ENVIRONMENTAL NEWSLETTER—Published quarterly, this includes UK and EC legislation and policy updates. It also incorporates news and information on the CBI's Environment Business Forum. It is available free of charge by sending your name, position, and company name to the editor at: Confederation of British Industry, Centre Point, 103 New Oxford Street, London WC1A 1DU. 071 379 7400.